W9-ASG-172

Twayne's United States Authors Series

Sylvia E. Bowman, *Editor*

INDIANA UNIVERSITY

Peter Taylor

PETER TAYLOR

By ALBERT J. GRIFFITH
Our Lady of the Lake College

Twayne Publishers, Inc. :: New York

Copyright © 1970 by Twayne Publishers, Inc.
All Rights Reserved

Library of Congress Catalog Card Number: 70-110713

813.54
T245G

MANUFACTURED IN THE UNITED STATES OF AMERICA

To Elizabeth

74812

Preface

PETER TAYLOR has possibly come as close as any writer now living to achieving the unanimous critical approval of those—however few—who read him. His very first stories submitted to the *Southern Review* in 1936 impressed Robert Penn Warren as "obviously the work of a very gifted writer who had a flavor and a way of his own." His published books—five collections of short stories, one novella, and one play—have received uniformly favorable reviews. The *Virginia Quarterly Review* pronounced him "an impeccable stylist" who produced "demonstrably superior work"; the *New York Herald Tribune* called him "possibly the most interesting and accomplished new writer to have come out of the South" in a decade; the *New York Times* insisted that he was "an authentic genius" and that the publication of a book of his was "a literary event of first importance"; the *San Francisco Chronicle* labeled him "a new major writer of American fiction."[1]

Retrospective critics and literary historians have been as laudatory as the initial reviewers. The first critic to undertake a detailed analysis of his work—Kenneth Clay Cathey in the *Western Review* (Autumn, 1953)—found him "among the most promising of our newer writers," an artist of self-imposed limitations whose writing revealed "an almost uninterrupted improvement in both technique and content." One of the latest critics, Morgan Blum in *Sewanee Review* (Autumn, 1962), viewing the productions of an additional ten years, finds that Taylor's development has not removed the self-imposed limitations but has nevertheless made him "one of the few writers to approach Tolstoy's talents" in several significant respects. Three recent critical surveys of current Southern literature provide typical comments: Richard K. Meeker calls Taylor "the most distinguished product so far" of the second-generation Vanderbilt school; John M. Bradbury cites Taylor's command of the short story medium as comparable "only with that of Katherine Anne Porter and Eudora Welty"; and Walter Sullivan unequivocally praises Taylor as "a perceptive artist, a skillful craftsman, and . . . the only American of his generation whose work can stand comparisons with that of Frank O'Connor and Chekhov and Joyce."

And yet, for all this unanimity of critical opinion, it is all too true that Peter Taylor is (as Blum put it) one of America's "most underrated" as well as one of America's "finest" writers. For the fact remains that, however much those who read him admire him, Peter Taylor is still relatively unknown not only to the bulk of the American reading public but to the majority of critics and historians of contemporary literature. Except to loyal readers of the *New Yorker* and a few aficionados of Southern literature, Peter Taylor is largely an unknown quantity.

The explanation for the paradox possibly lies in the peculiar American attitude toward the literary form which has been Peter Taylor's special province: the short story. Though American writers from Washington Irving to John Updike have proved themselves masters of the genre, there is not a single writer to achieve first-class literary recognition and only a few—O. Henry, perhaps, is the best known—to reach even a second- or third-class recognition on the basis of the short story alone. Among Taylor's fellow Southerners, for instance, there are Katherine Anne Porter, Eudora Welty, Carson McCullers, Truman Capote, and Flannery O'Connor, who have all done their most distinguished work in the short story form but have achieved important public and critical notice only through their novels.

Peter Taylor, unfortunately for his claim to fame, has never ventured far enough afield from his fruitful but narrow territory, the short story. His one book-length fiction so far is a novella of only thirty thousand words, not enough to attract the notice of those who can't help posing a geometric ratio between size and significance. Unfortunately, too, for his reputation, Taylor's themes and techniques have not been the artistically faddish ones which command the most attention today. The title originally given to one of his stories pretty well sums up his chief subjects: "Cousins, Family Life, Family Love, All That." Furthermore, as J. F. Powers has noted, Taylor refuses "to exploit his material to the limit";[2] his favorite method is the digressive-progressive memoir story which leisurely builds characterizations and releases the meaning in a situation without any great show of effects.

The purpose of this book, then, is to survey the work of Peter Taylor to try to see just what it does contain to make comparisons to James, Tolstoy, and Porter justified, as well as what it contains to make Peter Taylor unique. After a brief biographical introduction in the first chapter, each of Taylor's books is discussed in succeeding chapters. Because Taylor's works are not well known, the method will be to give an idea of the content and form of each story, with rather free use of direct quotation. A final chapter will try to suggest what Peter Taylor's most important achievement may be.

ALBERT J. GRIFFITH

Our Lady of the Lake College
San Antonio, Texas

Acknowledgments

I am greatly indebted to Peter Taylor, who has given me permission to quote from his works and who has graciously assisted me in assembling biographical information. For valuable information from the archives of Kenyon College, I am also indebted to Peter G. Edwards, director of public relations at Kenyon.

I am also grateful to the administration of Our Lady of the Lake College for varying kinds of assistance; to Sister Margaret Rose Warburton and Professor Perry E. Gragg, who read and criticized preliminary drafts; to Misses Linda Calia, Linda Lopez, Mary Otto, and Linda Jo Patak, who typed the manuscript; and to Professor Sylvia Bowman, who edited it.

I wish to make further acknowledgement to the following:

To Astor-Honor, Inc. for permission to quote from *A Long Fourth and Other Stories*, copyright, 1940, 1941, 1945, 1946, 1947, 1948, by Peter Taylor; *A Woman of Means*, copyright, 1948, 1949, 1950, by Peter Taylor; *The Widows of Thornton*, copyright, 1948, 1949, 1950, 1951, 1954, by Peter Taylor; *Tennessee Day in St. Louis: A Comedy*, copyright, 1955, 1956, 1957, by Peter Taylor; *Happy Families Are All Alike*, copyright, 1959, by Peter Taylor; *Miss Leonora When Last Seen and Fifteen Other Stories*, copyright, 1948, 1949, 1950, 1951, 1954, 1960, 1961, 1963, by Peter Taylor.

To Alfred A. Knopf, Inc. for permission to quote from Oswald Spengler, *The Decline of the West*, translated by Charles Francis Atkinson, Volume II, copyright, 1928, by Alfred A. Knopf, Inc.

Acknowledgements

Contents

Chronology

1917 Peter Taylor born, January 8, in Trenton, Tennessee, on ninth wedding anniversary of his parents, Matthew Hillsman Taylor (1884-1965) and Katherine Baird (Taylor) Taylor (1886-).

1920 Future wife, Eleanor Ross, born in Norwood, North Carolina.

1924 Moved to Nashville.

1926 Moved to St. Louis, Missouri, where father became president of an insurance company.

1926-1929 Attended Miss Rossman's School in St. Louis.

1929-1932 Attended St. Louis Country Day School.

1932 Moved to Memphis. Attended Memphis Central High School.

1935 Graduated from high school. Worked way to England on freighter during summer.

1936 Took courses under Allen Tate at Southwestern at Memphis in spring semester. Started at Vanderbilt in fall under John Crowe Ransom; became friend of Randall Jarrell.

1937 Dropped out of college and sold real estate (after Ransom left Vanderbilt for Kenyon College). Published first two stories in *River*.

1938-1940 Entered Kenyon in fall of 1938; became friend of Robert Lowell; graduated in spring of 1940; briefly enrolled as graduate student at Louisiana State University under Robert Penn Warren and Cleanth Brooks in fall of 1940. Sold poem to *Kenyon Review* and three stories to *Southern Review*.

1941-1945 Served in United States Army at Fort Ogelthorpe, Georgia, and at Tidworth Camp in England; discharged as sergeant.

1943 Married Eleanor Ross at St. Andrew's School chapel, Monteagle, Tennessee, on June 4.

1946-1948 Taught at Woman's College of University of North Carolina, Greensboro.

1948-1949 Assistant professor at Indiana University, Bloomington.

1948 First book, *A Long Fourth,* published in March. First child, Katherine Baird Taylor, born September 30. First association with *New Yorker* began with "Middle Age" (later titled "Cookie") in November 6 issue.

1949-1952 Returned to Woman's College of University of North Carolina at Greensboro.

1950 *A Woman of Means* published in May. Guggenheim Fellowship for 1950-51.

1952 Taught at University of Chicago in spring. Received National Institute of Arts and Letters grant. Returned to Kenyon College as associate professor in English and drama.

1953-1959 Advisory editor to *Kenyon Review.*

1954 *The Widows of Thornton* published in May.

1955 Second child, Peter Ross Taylor, born February 7. Fulbright grant to do research in Paris in 1955-56. Lectured at Fourth Conference on American Studies at Oxford.

1956 Returned to Kenyon.

1957 Premiere of *Tennessee Day in St. Louis* held at Kenyon, April 24-27; text of play published by Random House. Joined Ohio State University as associate professor to teach from January to June each year.

1958 Spent summer and fall in Italy with Robert Jarrell and Robert Fitzgerald.

1959 *Happy Families Are All Alike* published in November. "Venus, Cupid, Folly and Time" awarded O. Henry first prize.

1960 Ohioana Book Award to *Happy Families.* Wife's volume of poetry, *Wilderness of Ladies,* published.

1961 Ford Foundation Fellowship to study at Royal Court repertory theater in London for year.

1962 *Happy Families* published as paperback reprint by Lippincott.

1963 Rejoined University of North Carolina at Greensboro as professor of English, teaching fiction writing.

1964 Visiting professor at Harvard in fall.

1965 Awarded Rockefeller Foundation grant to take 1966-67 year away from teaching duties to devote full time to writing.

1966 Gave lecture on Randall Jarrell in Hopwood Lecture Series, University of Michigan.

1967 Joined English Department at the University of Virginia, Charlottesville. With Robert Lowell and Robert Penn Warren, edited memorial volume, *Randall Jarrell, 1914-1965.*

1968 Published new play, *A Stand in the Mountain,* in *Kenyon Review.* Worked on collected stories for Farrar, Straus & Giroux. Continued work on projected novel trilogy and a group of plays.

1969 Elected to membership in the National Institute of Arts and Letters in March. *Collected Stories* published in October.

CHAPTER 1

The Measure of Peter Taylor's World

I *"Tennessee Is a State of Mind"*

THOUGH PETER TAYLOR was born in a little country town in Tennessee, he wasn't reared there, and he never went back there to live. These biographical facts help to define the peculiar mixture of sentiment and irony which characterizes Peter Taylor's vision of his native region.[1] For, though his Southern agrarian birthright has always loomed large in his imagination, it has been like some legacy held in trust. It has been something he could use but not fully possess and certainly not dispose of. And, as a result, Peter Taylor has been, of all the brilliant talents in the Southern Literary Renaissance, the one most capable of seeing Southern culture simultaneously both as insider and as outsider.

The country town Peter Taylor came from is Trenton, Tennessee, a town known for little more than the pastoral serenity of its maple-lined streets. Located in the old Chickasaw country of West Tennessee, Trenton is a county seat and a local trading center for the cotton farmers of the area. It is the obvious model for the fictional town of Thornton, the point of origin of numerous characters in about a dozen of Taylor's works, and it may also contribute some features to the imaginary towns of Lovell, Braxton, and Thomasville in other stories.

Peter Taylor lived in Trenton only seven years. Born January 8, 1917, on the ninth wedding anniversary of his parents, he was the youngest of the four children of Hillsman and Katherine Taylor and the one who would have the least contact with his place of origin. The family's first move was to Nashville in 1924; then it moved to St. Louis, Missouri, in 1926; and finally to Memphis, Tennessee, in 1932. Taylor's formative years consequently were not spent in a country town but in large urban centers, both in and out of the South, where old patterns of behavior were giving way to new. Perhaps the most important phase of Taylor's life—the period between the ages of nine and fifteen—was spent not in the South at all, but in the Midwestern metropolis of St. Louis. "To my brother and sisters, as to my parents, the period in St. Louis represents a relatively brief interlude in their lives," Peter Taylor makes his narrator say in a recent story. "They are vague about a lot of things there that are very clear in my mind and they will ask me to refresh their memories about people and addresses and even events that took place in that period. For me, of course, almost the reverse is true since I lived there during those years of life when one is taking his measure of the world."[2]

The young Peter Taylor did not really leave behind the Southern way of life when he left the South itself. As so many of his own works testify, Southern families in exile carried with them many of the traditional patterns they had followed at home. Often bringing along their Negro servants and dependent kinfolk, these transplanted Southerners would try to live their old roles in the new environment, making only minimal adaptations and ignoring unpleasant incongruities. Taylor has one of his characters in *Tennessee Day in St. Louis* preparing a speech with the title, "Tennessee Is a State of Mind." The phrase is a particularly apt summary of the lasting influence of Southern culture on those who have once experienced it. "Ah, sometimes," the same Taylor character observes, "the Southerners one meets out of the South seem more Southern than the South." Always in the memories of these exiles, at any rate, was the image of the rural society on which they based what certainties they still retained.

Taylor's own family unquestionably had a vivid past to remember.[3] Both of his grandfathers were lawyers and politicians, and both, coincidentally, were named Robert Taylor. The more famous of the two was his mother's father, Robert Love ("Bob") Taylor of Happy Valley, Tennessee, a legend in his own lifetime. A United States Congressman (1879-81), a three-term governor of the state (1887-89, 1889-91, and 1897-99), and finally a United States Senator (1907-12), Bob Taylor was a practical joker, a renowned spinner of tall tales, and a wily vote-getter—all in the tradition of another eminent Tennessean, Davy Crockett. Governor Bob's most famous campaign was the 1886 race for the governorship, which found him, as the Democratic nominee, pitted against his brother, Alf Taylor, the Republican nominee. To this day, wry stories are still told about the two brothers stumping the state together, telling tales, fiddling, and pulling tricks on each other, in what came to be called Tennessee's "War of the Roses." An interesting footnote to this bit of Taylor family history is the fact that the prohibition cause also had a token candidate for governor that year: former Congressman and former Commissioner of Indian Affairs Nathaniel Green Taylor—Peter Taylor's great grandfather, the father of Bob and Alf. And, while Bob was the victor in 1886, Alf Taylor had his turn as governor thirty-five years later when he was seventy-three and had already served three terms as United States Congressman.

Though Governor Bob died five years before Peter Taylor was born, Governor Alf lived till 1931 when his grandnephew was fourteen. Probably stories about the one and recollections of the other contributed something to Peter Taylor's characterizations of Senator Caswell in *Tennessee Day in St. Louis* and of the imagined convention delegate in "The End of Play."

Peter Taylor's own father, Hillsman Taylor, also had a political career as a young man. Just three years after his graduation from Vanderbilt Law School, he served as speaker of the Tennessee House of Representatives. He was attorney general of the Thirteenth Judicial Circuit of Tennessee at the time Peter was born.

If the colorful world of the Southern politician became only a memory for the young Peter Taylor when Hillsman Taylor moved his family to St. Louis in 1926, it was nevertheless a carefully nurtured memory. Other interests, however, certainly took on new importance for Southern families transplanted to the Midwest. "We all came here to make money, you know, and came of our own free will," one of Peter Taylor's St. Louis characters says.

Hillsman Taylor, too, became a successful businessman in the big city. It was in St. Louis that the former country lawyer soon became president of the Missouri State Life Insurance Company and, as one of his major accomplishments, negotiated what was said to be the largest reinsurance deal of that day, involving three hundred million dollars worth of insurance and thirty-nine million dollars worth of assets. When, during the trough of the Depression, Hillsman Taylor decided to return to Tennessee, it was to new business interests in Memphis that he went, not back to the country law office in Trenton.

The kind of life Peter Taylor knew in St. Louis and Memphis can be inferred from the many stories in which he depicts families whose backgrounds are similar to his own.[4] For the children in these affluent families there are few hardships and many luxuries, including summer vacations in Michigan, dancing classes, gala parties, expensive gifts, and, of course, an ample supply of Negro servants. Only the Depression put a slight damper on their generally optimistic outlook. "If you were a worrier, as I was," one of Taylor's young protagonists says in "The Other Times," "it didn't seem possible that you would ever be able to make a living of the kind your father had always made." And in the background, associated with just such fears of failure, was the memory of the country town from which the family came and to which it might someday have to return.

Inside or outside the state, Peter Taylor's state of mind remained Tennessee.

II *The Years of Apprenticeship*

Hillsman Taylor had received his law degree from Vanderbilt University in 1906 and he hoped that his younger son would follow in his footsteps. That young son, however, had his own ideas about his education.[5] After attending Miss Rossman's private school in St. Louis and St. Louis Country Day School, Peter Taylor graduated from Memphis Central High School in 1935 with a scholarship to Columbia University. Perhaps his father's coolness to his Columbia aspirations had something to do with Peter's taking his departure from the family scene that summer by working his way to England on a freighter out of New Orleans. When he returned that fall, the dispute was unfortunately still not settled, with the result that the boy went nowhere until the spring semester of 1936.

The school Taylor finally enrolled in was Southwestern at Memphis, where he took English courses under Allen Tate. Though Tate left to take a position as a special lecturer in modern poetry at Columbia University the very next year, he advised his young student to go to the school his father had picked, Vanderbilt. There Taylor would have the opportunity to study under Tate's old mentor, John Crowe Ransom, the founder of the Fugitive group and the dean of the New Critics.

Taylor went on to Vanderbilt that fall, but he was doomed to another disappointment when Ransom moved the following year to Kenyon College in Gambier, Ohio. Virtually dropping out of college for a year (he took only a few courses as a special student at Southwestern), Taylor took a job selling real estate in Memphis. Not until the fall of 1938 did he transfer to Kenyon and resume his study under Ransom. Because he did badly in mathematics, a part of the pre-law curriculum, he was allowed by his father to concentrate his studies on literature.[6]

By the time he graduated from Kenyon in 1940, Peter Taylor already had published two short stories in the short-lived literary magazine, *River*, edited in Oxford, Mississippi, and a poem in the *Kenyon Review*. He next tried graduate work at Louisiana State University, studying under Robert Penn Warren and Cleanth Brooks. By this time, however, he knew his vocation was to be a fiction writer rather than a scholar, and he "dropped his courses and spent the year reading and writing fiction." Warren, who had earlier turned down the two stories later accepted by *River*, now took three of Taylor's stories ("A Spinster's Tale," "Sky Line," and "The Fancy Woman") for the *Southern Review;* and the literary career of Peter Taylor was officially launched.[7]

During these apprenticeship years, Taylor had come into contact with some of the most original and stimulating critical and creative minds in America. Since three of the most important of these—Ransom, Tate, and Warren—were leaders of the Agrarian movement, it is surprising that so little evidence of Agrarian thinking is found in Peter Taylor's writing.[8] Only one of his stories, "The Party" (1937), attempts to contrast the pastoral ideal so dear to the Agrarians with the urban-industrial reality; and it is an immature and mawkish story. Only one other story, "A Long Fourth" (1946), specifically alludes to the Agrarians; and it does so only when two of the Southern characters are deliberately burlesquing the Agrarian line to the embarrassment of a Yankee visitor. Of course, there are in Taylor's work many wistful references to "the old ways and the old teachings," to "the standards of a past era, a better era," to the former "atmosphere of a prosperous and civilized existence," and to the present sad corruption of the "traditions and institutions" of the country.[9] But these are not direct comments by the author; they are reflections of the thoughts of various characters, many of whom would gladly rally with the Agrarians against the urban-industrial menace. Taylor himself usually stands apart, not judging; he does, however, in "Miss Leonora When Last Seen" allow his gentle irony to prick those who "go on having sweet dreams" about preserving unspoilt the little country towns in which they themselves never actually live.

Ransom, Tate, and Warren undoubtedly had more influence on Taylor as literary critics and theorists than they had as Agrarians. As proponents of the New Criticism, all three were making important contributions to a revolution in literary study at the time Taylor had them as teachers. Tate's *Reactionary Essays on Poetry and Ideas,* for instance, appeared in 1936, the very year Peter Taylor was taking his courses at Southwestern. One of Ransom's most important critical works, *The World's Body,* was published in 1938, the year Peter Taylor followed him to Kenyon. And Robert Penn Warren and Cleanth Brooks's *Understanding Poetry* had been introduced to college classrooms also in 1938 and was making its first big impact about the time Taylor enrolled at Louisiana State.[10]

Henry James, of course, was the patron saint of all the New Critics; and Taylor must have been amply exposed to both Jamesian theory and to Jamesian practice by his literary mentors. In *The House of Fiction,* a 1950 short story anthology, for instance, Allen Tate and Caroline Gordon take their title and their epigraph from James, include stories by James and several Jamesian disciples, base their analyses of the stories on James's theories, and pack their bibliography with books by and about James. It is no wonder, then, that in the semi-autobiographical story "1939," Peter Taylor depicts his young Kenyon College hero as writing obvious imitations of Henry James. It is no wonder either that Taylor's most Jamesian book, *The Widows of Thornton,* should be dedicated to those disciples of the master, "Allen and Caroline."

All three of Taylor's famous teachers were more interested in poetry than they were in fiction; even Warren had written only one novel at the time of his association with Taylor. Moreover, Taylor's closest literary friends have been poets. Randall Jarrell, whom Taylor first met at Vanderbilt, was a faculty member at Kenyon when Taylor was there and has since been a colleague of Taylor's on the staff of the University of North Carolina at

Greensboro. The poet Robert Lowell came to Kenyon as a transfer student from Harvard the same year Taylor arrived, graduated with Taylor in the class of 1940, and went on to graduate work with him at Louisiana State.[11] It was Robert Lowell who acted as best man when Peter Taylor married Eleanor Ross of Norwood, North Carolina, who is also a publishing poet.[12]

Despite his close association with poets, Taylor himself has published only one poem.[13] That poem, "The Furnishings of a House," written during his undergraduate days, has an elevated diction and formal syntax that contrasts sharply with the colloquial style of his prose. It does reveal, however, that Taylor can exert a cold and stately discipline on his language when he wishes; and it suggests, therefore, that the seemingly undisciplined and artless effect of his prose style is only an illusion which his careful but quiet artistry makes possible. Certainly, the best of Peter Taylor's prose is very close to poetry—not so much in its intensity or compression, as in its feeling for the clean line, for the interrelationships of words in sequence, for the interlocking rhythms of sound and sense.

Peter Taylor was fortunate in having a literary apprenticeship which so well prepared him for the task he was to set himself in his later fiction and plays.

III *"A Kind of Journeyman Writer"*

In the story "1939," Peter Taylor's first-person narrator depicts himself as a college teacher and writer who has enjoyed neither great financial success nor an extravagant literary reputation. "I stand before the class as a kind of journeyman writer, a type of whom Trollope might have approved," he says. "Yet this man behind the lectern is a man who seems happy in the knowledge that he knows—or thinks he knows—what he is about." Probably no better summation of Peter Taylor's own literary self-image could be given. From the start, he has known what he was about; and he has achieved through the years a high quality of work that has more than merited the approval it has consistently received.

The early start Taylor got when he began publishing as an undergraduate was offset to some extent by the slow-up World War II caused. Taylor entered the army as an enlisted man in

June, 1941; and he served two and a half years at Fort Ogelthorpe, Georgia (the setting for "Rain in the Heart"), before going overseas to Tidworth Camp in England. Assigned to the Rail Transportation Corps, Taylor rose to the rank of sergeant before his honorable discharge in December, 1945. In the meantime, he had married Eleanor Ross on June 4, 1943.[14]

Taylor began his academic career in 1946 when he took a post at the Woman's College of the University of North Carolina at Greensboro. Three times he has returned to the Greensboro school after teaching stints elsewhere: at Indiana University, 1948-49; at the University of Chicago, 1952, Kenyon College, 1952-57, and Ohio University, 1957-63; and at Harvard University, 1964. He now teaches writing at the University of Virginia in Charlottesville. During the summer of 1955, he gave several lectures on fiction at the Fourth Conference on American Studies in Great Britain, sponsored by the Department of State's International Educational Exchange Program, at University College, Oxford.

Though Taylor published one or two minor stories during the war years, it was only between 1945 and 1947 that he hit his stride again with stories in *Sewanee Review, Partisan Review,* and *Kenyon Review*. Between the end of the war and the publication of his first short-story collection, *A Long Fourth,* in 1948, he had also written two plays and a "long novelette." The critical reception to *A Long Fourth* was encouraging, so the novelette was published in 1950, under the title *A Woman of Means.* (Parts of the novel had been published previously in *Harper's Bazaar* and the *New Yorker.*) The association with the *New Yorker,* which began in 1948 with the story "Middle Age" (later entitled "Cookie"), became a close one over the years, with the *New Yorker* presenting twenty-two of Taylor's stories to date. Additional short story collections—*The Widows of Thornton, Happy Families Are All Alike, Miss Leonora When Last Seen,* and *Collected Stories*—were published in 1954, 1959, 1963, and 1969, and two full-length plays, *Tennessee Day in St. Louis* and *A Stand in the Mountains,* were published in 1957 and 1968, respectively.[15] While none of these books received very extensive critical attention, each received almost unanimous praise from those reviewers who did take notice. An unspectacular but steady pile of accolades and honors began to accumulate.

Nine different times, for instance, Taylor's stories have been selected for inclusion in Martha Foley's *Best American Short Story* annuals; four times they have been among the O. Henry prize stories. One story, "Venus, Cupid, Folly and Time," was included in both of the 1959 annuals, even winning the O. Henry first prize. Other honors include a *Partisan Review* award for "The Scoutmaster" in 1945 and the Ohioana Book Award to *Happy Families Are All Alike* in 1960. Taylor himself was awarded a Guggenheim Memorial Fellowship for 1950-51 and a one thousand dollar grant from the National Institute of Arts and Letters in 1952. Under a Fulbright grant in 1956, he was able to do research in Paris for a projected play on Confederate statesmen and other Southerners who settled in Paris after the Civil War; under a Ford Foundation Fellowship in 1961, he was able to spend a year at the Royal Court repertory theater in London studying theater techniques; and, finally, under a $13,500 Rockefeller Foundation grant in 1965, he was able to take the 1966-67 academic year away from teaching duties to devote full time to writing.

Despite all this professional recognition, Taylor still considers himself an old-fashioned amateur who writes for fun without much apparent method. He works on several things at the same time, he once told an interviewer;[16] and he files away a story when he gets stuck. He usually produces four or five stories a year, often taking as long as three weeks for the initial page, but finishing the remainder of the story in only a few days. "Actually, I suppose I'm outlining in my head those first weeks," he says. Taylor also enjoys acquiring real estate and refurbishing old houses. Among his purchases have been an apartment house in Greensboro, an old farmhouse built by one of his wife's ancestors soon after the Revolution in Norwood, another old home in Hillsboro, and just lately a log cabin on an old mountain farm in Virginia. Peter Taylor is, as might be guessed from his favorite subject matter, a family man, who dedicates his books to his parents, his wife, and his two children, Katherine Baird Taylor and Peter Ross Taylor.

The significance of Peter Taylor's life, however, does not lie in the bare biographical details about a "journeyman writer." The significance is in the vision that his life produced and in the fully realized works of literary art which embody that vision.

CHAPTER 2

A Long Fourth

I *"The Old Ways and the Old Teachings"*

"The Scoutmaster," the first story in Peter Taylor's initial volume, *A Long Fourth*,[1] epitomizes in many ways the themes and techniques that dominate Taylor's early stories and remain influential in the work of his later career. It not only introduces his favorite subject matter of urban Southern upper-middle-class domestic life and his favorite narrative method of the conversational digressive-reflective family chronicle, it also dramatizes basic insights about time, change, and cultural roles which receive frequent corroboration in his other works.

An awareness of time is present in "The Scoutmaster" from the first word until the last. The first-person narrator harkens back to the central events of the story—events which took place when he was about ten years old—from a position in the present time which gives perspective to these long ago incidents. "That year all the young people in Nashville were saying, 'Don't tell me that, old dear, because it makes me *too* unhappy,'" the story begins, locating the action in a specific temporal context. But the time of the story is not just "that year," probably in the late 1920's, in which certain incidents occurred. It is also the unspecified present from which the past is being viewed. It is the more remote past of historical record, the times through which the narrator's father and uncles have lived, for instance, and of romantic legend, what Uncle Jake refers to as "the golden days when a race of noble gentlemen and gracious ladies inhabited the land of the South." And it is also the durative contour of time in which the discrete units of the calendar are indistinguishable.

Philosophically, time may be described as a concept forced on man's consciousness by the evidence of change, by the operation of the principle of mutability in his physical environment. And it is thus that time impinges on the consciousness of the characters in "The Scoutmaster," for change is evident all about them. Some of the changes, though trivial in themselves, are disturbing to the characters as symptomatic of much larger changes which they sense but cannot name. The father, for instance, cannot "abide" his teenage daughter's slang expressions; the mother complains of her too "liberal" use of makeup.

If there is an inexplicable reluctance to tolerate the ephemeral fads which a new generation adopts, there is often an even greater (if hardly more explicable) reluctance to accept the more permanent changes which time brings in personal circumstances. Death is, of course, the chief of these changes and the hardest to accept. Uncle Jake, for one, has never fully adjusted to the deaths of his parents, of his brother Louis, or of his wife and daughter. "If only Margaret, herself, had lived to make him and Presh a home, he might not have forever been looking to the past and being so uncritical of things in the present," the narrator's father says, adding: "He might have taken hold of himself."

Other changes, not so irrevocable as death, are nevertheless disconcerting in their own ways. The family finds it difficult to accept relatives' changes in religion, occupation, or marital status. Even the developing emotions of a child or adolescent can cause family upsets, as when Virginia Ann surprises Uncle Jake by responding with hurt feelings to his playful teasing about a boy friend or when the young narrator once reacted "in a beastly rage" to a practical joke by Uncle Jake.

The most crucial changes, however, are not so much those which involve physical circumstances as those which involve moral values. Such changes are often of culture-wide occurrence, but they are most frequently recognized only as they are manifested in individuals. The central incident of "The Scoutmaster" is a dramatization of this kind of change and its effects on the family circle. The denouement occurs when the adult members of the family, returning home early from a rainy Thanksgiving Day football game, discover that the teenage daughter and her date had never even left for the game, but had remained at home, where they are found together on the living room sofa. The boy friend is driven from the house, the daughter is banished to her room, and the entire family is plunged into a state of shock and depression.

The tense situation is keenly felt but only vaguely understood by the preadolescent narrator, who, as the only potential chaperone left at home in the absence of his parents, has been a kind of unwitting and unwilling accomplice to his sister's indiscretion. The boy must take his cues from the older members of the family: from Brother, who confides disturbedly, "Well, they were only necking, but they sure were *at* it"; from Mother and Father, who try to distract themselves with cards and conversation; and finally from Uncle Jake, who makes an impromptu but heartfelt speech at a Boy Scout meeting later that evening.

From this episode, the narrator learns something of the relationship between changes in cultural values and the roles which people play in their daily lives. He already has an awareness that certain members of the family fill fairly clearly defined roles. "I would have said my mother's function was Motherhood and my father's Fatherhood," he notes at one point, only to learn later from his mother that the process of change makes their roles more complex. When his mother and father enter fully into their marital roles by shutting out all others from their conversations, it seems to the narrator as if they have "left their bodies" and passed beyond his ken.

In the course of the story, too, the narrator comes to recognize that the divorced aunt who brought her gaiety into their house for a short sojourn also filled a role. When Aunt Grace makes her departure, the young nephew senses a new truth, while gazing in "breathtaking amazement" at her appearance:

> I felt myself growing timid in her presence, for she had become a stranger to me. . . . And all those things that indicated that Aunt Grace was one sort of person now indicated that she was quite another sort. She was not the utterly useless if wonderfully ornamental member of the family. In the solid blueness of her eyes I was surely on the verge of finding some marvelous function for her personality. . . . I was about to find the reason why there should be one member of a boy's family who was wise or old-fashioned enough to sit with Mother and Father and discuss the things they could not abide in Virginia Ann and yet who was foolish or newfangled enough to enjoy the very things that Virginia Ann called "the last word." (7-8)

The mystery to the narrator is the role to be attributed to Uncle Jake, the gentle widower whose wistful nostalgia suffuses the household. Jake has none of Aunt Grace's newfangledness; he remains essentially "old-fashioned." The narrator's father articulates a truth about Jake which the narrator will discover for himself at the climax of the story: "He's really incapable of being very realistic about his dealing with people. His real calling, his real profession is, you know, that of the Scoutmaster. It's during those Thursday night meetings with the boys that poor Jake fulfills himself."

The Joycean epiphany which confirms this truth for the narrator comes at the scout meeting the night of Virginia Ann's disgrace. Brought along to the meeting so that he will be removed from the tense family situation for a while, the young narrator watches the unfamiliar ritualistic activity of the scout meeting transform the familiar friends of his brother into "total strangers." He feels "a kind of elevation" as he hears the lists of adjectives—"loyal, brave, trustworthy, clean, reverent"—recited in the scout oath. Then, gradually, Uncle Jake, "losing himself in the role of the eternal Scoutmaster," becomes a "stranger," too.

> I realized now that Father had been right. This was Uncle Jake fulfilling himself. And to fulfill one's self was to remove one's self somehow beyond the reach of my own understanding and affection. It seemed that the known Uncle Jake had moved out of his body just as Aunt Grace had moved out of hers when she sang and laughed and as the Mother and Father whose hands I liked to have placed gently on the top of my head left their bodies whenever they excluded all the world from their conversation. (30)

The "exclusion of all the world" is the inevitable concomitant of all role-playing, the narrator at last understands; and, when Uncle Jake, "the last human soul" to whom he might "turn" in a person-to-person relationship, becomes a "stranger" playing a "role," he feels himself "deserted." But this sense of isolation and alienation which the child feels, as bit by bit he comes to adopt the adult method of identifying individuals as roles instead of persons, is only part of the revelation of this story. In addition, "The Scoutmaster" discriminates the special character of the kind of role which Jake has been destined to play.

This priest-prophet role, symbolized by the scoutmaster's functions of conducting rituals and of sermonizing in support of traditional values, is something "more serious" than the artist-clown "laughter and song" role of Aunt Grace and "more relentless" even than the parent-spouse education and ministration role of the mother and father. "Half ridiculous and half frightening" in his scout uniform, Uncle Jake performs with deadly solemnity the haruspical task which the mysterious changes of time perennially call for:

> In that cold, bare, bright room he was saying that it was our great misfortune to have been born in these latter days when the morals and manners of the country had been corrupted, born in a time when we could see upon the members of our own families—upon our own sisters and brothers and uncles and aunts—the effects of our failure to cling to the teachings and ways of our forefathers. And he was saying that it was our duty and great privilege, as Boy Scouts, to preserve those honorable things which were left from the golden days when a race of noble gentlemen and gracious ladies inhabited the land of the South. He was saying that we must preserve them until one day we might stand with young men from all over the nation to demand a return to the old ways and the old teachings everywhere. (30-31)

The old ways and the old teachings—these are in some way the subject of all the remaining stories in *A Long Fourth.* Peter Taylor asks many questions about his cultural heritage as a Southerner. Which of the traditional values matter most? How are they affected by time and change? What allegiance is owed to them? How are they to be evaluated against present conditions?

Characteristically, Peter Taylor presents these problems as they confront the evolving consciousness of a child or a young adult approaching a new level of maturity. As in James Joyce, the youthful protagonist comes to terms with his beliefs and values by a series of epiphanies through which something of their essential significance is made manifest. In Peter Taylor, however, the resolution the protagonist reaches is not rejection of, or flight from, tradition, but some sort of accommodation with it, some sort of adjustment of present experience to the legacy of the past.

II *"The Changed View From the Window"*

Two stories of this first volume, "Sky Line" and "A Spinster's Tale," take up in particular the reactions of sensitive children to the disturbing threats which time's changes pose to their domestic security. Written in 1939 and 1938, respectively, these two stories, the earliest pieces included in *A Long Fourth,* reveal the long-time concern Taylor has had for this theme. "Sky Line," the less artificial of the two stories, both of which are marred by self-conscious literary techniques, is especially Joycean in form—provoking comparisons to the famous opening montages of *A Portrait of the Artist as a Young Man.* The story is a series of fifteen chronological sections detailing important impressions of the boy protagonist as he passes from the innocent wonderment of childhood to the world-weary resignation of a precocious adulthood. Besides the presence of the boy Jimmy, the episodes are linked by several symbols emphasizing the changes of time.

The first of these symbols is the swaying vine-baskets which the boy's grandmother had hung on the porch. "Is it God knocking?" Jimmy asks in the first line of the story as he hears the wind blowing the baskets against the house. "No, no. That isn't God. That isn't God," an adult, probably his mother, answers him. This answer, however, is ironic; for, in the total context of the story, the answer should be, "Yes. That is God. That is the hand of the Prime Mover heard signalling the passage of time."

Like everything else which bombards the senses of the developing child, the swinging wire baskets leave their indelible mark on the consciousness—a mark graphically represented by the chipped-off paint on the clapboard siding of the porch against which the baskets knocked for many years. Even after the grandmother is dead, the baskets removed, and the house repainted, Jimmy does not forget the clattering of the baskets which he will ever associate with his grandmother and with the primeval innocence of that period of his childhood before the religious mystery of death intruded; the "sunken places" beneath the new paint remain to remind him "ever after" of those years.

A second key symbol is the one singled out for emphasis in the title: the changing sky line of the neighborhood in which the boy lives. In the days of the swinging baskets, the suburb is largely undeveloped. But, where once there were only Jimmy's house, the house on the corner, and the speckled stucco next door where a little girl lived, soon there are new houses "scattered along the winding streets and along his own block." The colored "For Sale" signs disappear as a new Catholic church with a yellow brick tower and a new public school building go up in vacant lots where the high yellow grass once looked to the boy like "the central plains of Africa." Later on there is a new drugstore on a nearby corner, and later still tall apartment houses appear on the horizon.

The new buildings are the irrefutable evidence of change for the boy; even when he sometimes feels that something isn't "completely changed," he is kept away from it by another feeling that it "isn't as it has been." Strangely, it is not so much the effect of change as the process itself which disturbs him: "Things have changed in the suburb; repeatedly he has told the new children how things once were, he is that conscious of it; but something forever keeps him from trying to observe too closely just how the new buildings go up." And, despite the burgeoning skyline, Jimmy is ever mindful of prior states, content to think of "other wallpapers that he remembers" on the wall of a room or pleased to reflect "that under the paint the marks that the vine-baskets made are actually still there."

Also symbolic are the erosive forces of nature, the wind and especially the rain. The yellow light that precedes or follows a change in weather generally accompanies the major discoveries of the story. After the grandmother's funeral, for instance, "everything outside the living room window looks yellowish" and the "rain comes like a burst of tears." When the rivalry of the boy's father and the little neighbor girl's father manifests itself in a vicious game of catch one day, dark clouds gather until the afternoon light turns yellow and rain streams down like a waterfall. It is in the rain that the boy, a little older, catches the illness which gives him the delirious dream of his father and the little girl's mother "dead on the streetcar tracks"; and it is in the rain that, grown older still, he discovers the true relationship between his now-widowed father and the little girl's mother and visualizes "the dark scene on his mother's guest room bed." And, in the final scene of the story, the light of the afternoon is described as "yellow," even "bilious," when the boy learns of his father's marriage to the little girl's mother, right before "rain bursts upon him" and drives him to the final epiphany in the room of the little girl.

The central image of the story is perhaps the house itself, the center of the boy's growth and development. Apparently belonging to the grandmother in the days of the undeveloped skyline, passed on to the boy's mother who must struggle to keep it during the hard days of the depression, and finally inherited by the boy himself, the house clearly represents the security of the past threatened by forces from within and without. Through its windows Jim sees the changes take place around him. Two such scenes are especially relevant. In the first, Jim, secure behind the black-wire screen in his upstairs room, watches the little neighbor girl bobbing up and down in the round zinnia bed below on the day of her father's funeral. In the second, the positions of the two are reversed: the girl is behind the screen at the upstairs window in what is now her own room, and Jim is down below in the zinnia bed. But, in the interval between the two scenes, much has happened: the little girl and her mother have auctioned off their furniture and moved in with Jim's family, Jim's father has lost his job and the little girl's mother has gone to work, Jim himself has been seriously ill and his mother has died, Jim has been moved to his father's room and the now adolescent little girl has been moved into his, Jim's father and the little girl's mother have become first business associates and then lovers and now husband and wife, and most significantly of all, as Jim's security has decreased and the little girl's increased, Jim has overtaken her in worldly understanding so that the older girl seems to have "the innocence of someone years younger than himself, the innocence of a very little girl."

This final scene is charged with conflict, as pubescent sexuality brings the boy and girl together in the house deserted by their honeymooning parents. The boy has watched the encroachments of the girl and her mother in his family circle, and he has seen his father and his mother each made into a "different person" by their acceptance of this outside force. Now, as he stands bare-chested and wet with rain before the sluttish girl wiggling seductively in her negligee, he must decide whether he too will finally succumb:

> The rain falls outside the open window, and now and again a raindrop splashes through the screen onto his face. At last it is almost night when the rain stops, and if there is any unnatural hue in the light, it is green. His heart has stopped pounding now, and all the heat has gone from his face. He has heard the hanging baskets beat against the house and felt the silence after their removal. He has heard the baseball smacking in the wet gloves of the men and seen the furniture auctioned on the lawn. The end of his grandmother, the defeat of his mother, the despair of his father, and the resignation of his new stepmother are all in his

> mind. The remarkable thing in the changed view from the window which had once been his lies in the tall apartment houses which punctuate the horizon and in the boxlike, flat-roofed ones in his own neighborhood. Through this window the girl too, he knows, must have beheld changes. (106)

His decision, however, emerges from these thoughts; and, when he turns back to the girl, it is evident that he will not capitulate. Though all is quietly understated here, the theme seems to be clear: change must be accommodated, but it need not be embraced.

III *"The Beastly Vision"*

Unlike "Sky Line," "A Spinster's Tale" covers a period of only a few months; but it is also a story of disturbing change, and it too marks a passage from childhood to adulthood. In this instance, the protagonist is a young girl, just entering her teens, who faces change in a form more frightening and grotesque than the subtle and insinuating form which the boy faces in "Sky Line." "A Spinster's Tale," as the title suggests, is a first-person narrative: the retrospective account of the young girl now turned spinster. The action runs from October to May in an unspecified year, presumably around the turn of the century, in Nashville. The setting is again a family home—this time an old-fashioned and "shadowy" and "brutally elegant" town house with stained-glass windows, mosaic hearth, full-length mirror panels by the windows, beaded lampshades, cavernous hallways, red-carpeted stairways, and grandfather clocks.

The tale begins on the day, just a few months after her mother's death, that the young narrator, Elizabeth, first notices a neighborhood drunkard, Mr. Speed, passing by her house. At this time, Elizabeth is an innocent fairy-tale child, idly trying out chairs in the parlor like Goldilocks or peering in mirrors "trying to discover a resemblance between [herself] and the wondrous Alice who walked through a looking-glass." It is just as she is saying the magic wish-words "Away, away" to herself in the mirror that her vision slips from the mirror to the window and to the terrifying sight of Mr. Speed "walking like a cripple with one foot on the curb and one in the street."

What was there about the drunken old man that made Elizabeth "dry-eyed" in fright? Nowhere does Taylor explicitely state the symbolism of Mr. Speed, but he provides numerous clues throughout the story to suggest that Mr. Speed is the dreamlike projection of some unbridled masculine principle which the motherless girl unconsciously fears and resents. In the first place, Mr. Speed is closely associated in the girl's mind with the other males who surround her: with her eighteen-year-old brother, whose teenage carousing inspires Puritanic predictions of eternal damnation; with her father and uncles, whose toddy drinking in the parlor produces a merry camaraderie the girl cannot broach; and with the young Benton boys (friends of her brother), whose horseless carriage seems an invitation to wild adventure.

The girl Elizabeth is aware of these links herself. The opening sentence of her story is a comparison of her fear *for* her brother with her fear *of* Mr. Speed, and later she puts into words the thought that in her brother and father she saw "something of Mr. Speed." Significantly, she adds: "And I knew that it was more than a taste for whisky they had in common." Later, she observes something in her brother's and her father's "nature" that was "fully in sympathy with the very brutality" of Mr. Speed's drunkenness. Her reactions to various happenings make it clear that a domineering male sexuality is a principal basis for this identification. Thus, the scene in which Elizabeth detains and beguiles her drunken brother in her bedroom is a preparation for the scene of the final confrontation with Mr. Speed, the action of which it helps to motivate. For Elizabeth will not allow herself to reflect too long about her "feelings" for her brother—"my desire for him to strike me and my delight in his natural odor"—feelings which derive from her own burgeoning adolescence and her unguided attempts to establish her own sexual identity.

That Elizabeth's attitude towards Mr. Speed is also affected by her sexual feelings is revealed by her thoughts the very first time she spies him, when she has a "sudden inexplicable memory" of her mother on her deathbed, apparently the victim of complications from the delivery of a stillborn baby. Though Elizabeth dwells only on the pleasant aspects of the memory (the warmth of her mother's cheek against hers) and represses the unpleasant (the mother suddenly sending her from the room and beckoning the nurse), the inference seems inevitable that she associates Mr.

Speed subconsciously with the cause of her mother's death: with the male principle to which her mother submitted in pregnancy.

Futhermore, Elizabeth resents the "blustering tone of merry tolerance" with which her father and her uncles indulgently refer to Mr. Speed's drunken antics and the vulgar disdain with which her father refuses to hear of her fear of Mr. Speed. Her father, in fact, after giving her some sententious advice becomes in her eyes a kind of Mr. Speed himself: "He punched at his left side several times, gave a prolonged belch, settled a pillow behind his head, and soon was sprawled beside me on the settee, snoring." Elizabeth also thinks of Mr. Speed at other significant times. Hearing her father talk about hundreds of soldiers in the Union Depot before the Spanish-American War, she visualizes "all those men there, that close together" and finds it "something like meeting Mr. Speed in the front hall." And even a mental image of all the "pitiable" little girls in Miss Hood and Miss Herron's Belmont School "being called for by gentle ladies or warm-breasted Negro women" conjures up "the beastly vision of Mr. Speed." Finally, there is her association of Mr. Speed with a primordial symbol of virile power—a wild horse. The horse image first comes up when Elizabeth's brother tries to frighten her with a pointless anecdote: "I saw three horses running away out on Harding Road today! . . . They were running to beat hell and with little girls riding them!" It occurs again in the last line of the story when the Elizabeth of the present, commenting on her recurring memories of the Mr. Speed episode, notes that "It was only the other night that I dreamed I was a little girl on Church Street again and that there was a drunk horse in our yard." The significance of the image is made explicit, however, when Elizabeth comments to her brother:

> "I wouldn't mind him less if he were sober," I said. "Mr. Speed's like—a loose horse."
>
> This analogy convinced him. He knew then what I meant.
>
> "You mustn't waste your time being afraid of such things," he said in great earnestness. "In two or three years there'll be things to be afraid of. Things you really can't avoid." (118)

Not only does this passage point to Mr. Speed's oneiric meaning, it points to the underlying cause of the girl's anxieties: the changes which adolescence is bringing to her life. The situation becomes transparent in the dream Elizabeth has about a "little girl whose hands began to get very large." "Grown men came for miles around to look at the giant hands and to shake them," Elizabeth recounts; "but the little girl was ashamed of them and hid them under her skirt." At first, in the dream, Elizabeth is an onlooker who laughs uproariously at the little girl's fear; then she becomes the little girl. The recollection of the dream is juxtaposed with a recollection of the day Elizabeth's father gives her a dressing table for her birthday with the inscription "For my young lady daughter." That is on the same day that Elizabeth begins to put up her hair, adult-fashion, in a knot on the back of her head.

Aware of her own maturation, Elizabeth is consequently also aware that she cannot avoid Mr. Speed and all that he represents to her. She has an "intuitive knowledge that Mr. Speed is "a permanent and formidable figure" in her life which she will "be called upon to deal with"; eventually, she comes to accept his existence "as a natural part" of her life, though "something to be guarded against" or "to be thoroughly prepared for" when it comes to her door. By the time Mr. Speed does come to her door, Elizabeth has "done everything that a little girl, now fourteen, could do in preparation for such an eventuality," including taking her place as mistress in the motherless household. She experiences for the last time "the inconsolable desperation of childhood" at the moment that the drunken old man staggers through the rain to her porch; then, though one part of her longs to hide her face in the maternal bosom, another part of her makes her "deal with Mr. Speed, however wrongly."

The "dealing with" Mr. Speed is the denouement of the story. While the old reprobate petrifies the Negro maid with his phallic cane and his brutal oaths, Elizabeth acts out her inevitable role "with courage but without wisdom" and summons the police in the Black Maria to come get him. "I saw myself as a little beast adding to the injury that what was bestial in man had already done him," Elizabeth admits adding: "I was frightened by the thought of the cruelty which I found I was capable of, a cruelty which seemed inextricably mixed with what I had called courage."

Though Elizabeth has this insight into her own behavior, her decisive action at this point has already set the pattern for her whole life. By rejecting Mr. Speed and by refusing to minister to him when, knocked unconscious by a fall on the steps, he lies helpless before her in the beating rain, she rejects the uxorial and maternal role of womankind and dooms herself to spinsterhood. A conversation earlier in the story has prepared us for this:

> "What ever did happen to Speed's old maid sister?" my uncle the doctor said.
>
> "She's still with him," Father said. (124)

Like Speed's old maid sister, Elizabeth too remains ever bound to him, for she confides: "... despite the surge of pity I felt for the old man on our porch that afternoon, my hatred and fear of what he had stood for in my eyes have never left me. And since the day that I watched myself say 'away' in the mirror, not a week has passed but that he has been brought to my mind by one thing or another" (129). The title of the story, "A Spinster's Tale," is the confirmation of the reader's suspicions: unlike the protagonist of "Sky Line" who learns to cope successfully with the anxieties induced by time's changes, the unfortunate girl of this story, arresting her own development, withdraws into a solitary role where the speedy changes of life's cycle can no longer affect her.

IV *"The Sum of a Thousand Accidents"*

Though time's changes are perhaps most evident to children, the problems that the passage of time creates are not limited to those of growing up. Two of Peter Taylor's stories in *A Long Fourth*, "Allegiance" and "Rain in the Heart," dramatize problems all people have when they attempt to evaluate new experiences against norms drawn from the past. It is probably not coincidental that both of these stories are set in World War II—a period of violent change naturally conducive to the reassessment of traditional values.

The protagonist of "Allegiance" is a young soldier from Nashville brought by the exigencies of wartime into a situation he would probably never otherwise have faced—a situation where he must examine in person the subject of a family myth, a myth he has always previously taken at face value. The scene is London, a locale far removed from the parochial atmosphere of his familiar environment and, more significantly, from the all-pervasive influence of his mother's point of view. For this young man has, up to the moments recounted in the story, habitually accepted without question his mother's version of an incident in the past which led to the estrangement of his mother and her older sister, the young man's aunt. He has indeed a "heritage of resentment" against his elegant aunt, whom he believes to have "grievously wronged" his mother "in a manner so subtle and base" that he has never known or even wished to know its nature. He has moreover a "silent pact" with his now dead mother which forbids him even to hear the other side of the case as he might if he were to open his aunt's letters. He has in short an "allegiance" which he does not intend to betray.

The story opens, however, with the words "Come in," spoken by the aunt—words that are on one level a mere polite invitation to enter the aunt's apartment, but on another a summons to enter into another point of view. The young man is amazed that his aunt can "dare to presume" his acceptance of her bid, yet he acquiesces, albeit "with trepidation," afraid that he shall "yield" more than he wishes. The imagery suggests the archetypal encounter of the quest hero and the legendary enchantress. The aunt acknowledges to her soldier nephew, "You want only to accomplish your mission and get yourself home again," yet she is clearly concerned to win him over to herself. She is described as "still a great beauty," a woman of "charm" and "fascination" (her "romantic quality"), possessed of "a sort of mystical, superhuman ignorance" of her own activities but capable of enduring anything "to gain her ends." "I feel that I am in the presence of some newfangled sort of idolater and conjurer," the young man says as he listens to his aunt draw on her ageless memory to cast a spell of words by which she makes herself and her exotic den of a room seem to "constitute the only certainty." There is in her attitude the hint of "some magic potency to the mere actuality of the moment" and "to the sound of her own voice," and the young man feels "a sort of literal enchantment . . . where all the past and all the future and all occurrences of the exterior world are of no consequence."

In such circumstances, it is no wonder that the young man fears that he may at some point "betray someone or something." As the interview proceeds, the "uncertainties" of his mind increase; and he becomes unsure whether his consciousness of betrayal is of "a possibility or a fact." His guilty fear is crystallized in the moment when his eyes and those of the aunt meet for an instant in the mirror, and he hears the sound of their "commingled" laughter.

But what is it which is so subject to betrayal? As in so many other Peter Taylor stories, the question at issue is one concerning the significance of time. The young soldier has inherited from his mother not only her version of some past injury from the aunt, but her vision of time as well—a vision which underlies her interpretation of the past injury. Though the mother's view is nowhere articulated in the story, it can be inferred as the opposite of the aunt's view of time, a view which the young man explicitly discusses. His aunt, the nephew discerns, has a "concern only for what is actual," and she has a "faith in the actual's being but the sum of a thousand accidents." Thus to her mind, interpersonal relationships (such as the past one between herself and the young man's mother and the present one between herself and the young man) are the result of fortuitous compilations of circumstances rather than human volition. As the nephew understands her, she feels no responsibility for the past and no undue anxiety for the present, only a reliance on the happy arrangement of accidents.

Contrasted with this view is the history-burdened view of the mother who found nothing accidental in the past event which had caused her estrangement from her sister. From the young man's attitude toward the aunt, we can sense his inherited belief in human choice as the efficient cause of good and evil; he is both shocked and fascinated by the aunt's faith in accidents and longs to refute it. *"I have come here and glimpsed the unique sort of power and truth you have discovered or created,"* he manages to insinuate through his tone of voice, *"but now I wish to remain to disprove its worth."* Ironically, it is his own beliefs, not hers, which are brought into doubt, which are, in fact, almost betrayed in the charmed presence of his "complicated and worldly" aunt.

When the young narrator leaves the aunt's apartment, he is still awe-struck by the "fate" he might have met before the aunt's "absolute authority." He has escaped, somehow, the enchantress' final spell, but he has not escaped to freedom. Even though his mind remains "troubled by a doubt of the reality of all things" and "haunted for a while by an unthinkable distrust for the logic and rarefied judgments" of his dead mother, he feels himself "still a prisoner in her parlor in Nashville." His allegiance to the norm of the past, represented by his mother, is too deep-rooted to be dispelled even by the magic fascination of his foreign adventure.

The hero of "Rain in the Heart," the other World War II story in *A Long Fourth*, is also a young soldier from Tennessee who is brought into a position where he must reassess his traditional values. Both setting and situation are far more ordinary in this story, however, and the hero faces no antagonist so formidable as the aunt in "Allegiance." This time the soldier is a drill sergeant, stationed at a Southern army post (apparently Fort Oglethorpe, Georgia, just a few miles from Chattanooga, Tennessee), who has an overnight pass to permit him to visit his recent bride for the first time since their honeymoon. Enroute from drill field to barracks to bus to streetcar to furnished apartment, he has several encounters which lead him to a moment of deep reflectiveness about the "terrible unrelated diversity in things."

The sergeant is characterized at once as one who cherishes traditional values: home, family, romantic love, the good life, the beauty of nature, the heritage from the past. Even as he sets out on his journey to his bride, he carries with him a symbolic burden —"a big volume of Civil War history" from the city library. This "heavy, dark history book" puts into perspective for him not only the present war for which he is drilling rookies but also other aspects of the modern life. He is acutely aware, for instance, that the ridge where his bride has found an apartment is the site of a bloody Civil War battle—presumably, though it is not mentioned by name, the Battle of Chickamauga, where over sixteen thousand on each side were killed. He is sure, moreover, that if he had lived at the time of that battle he "would have seen ever so clearly the Cause for that fighting."

On his way, he picks up another symbolic item, a bouquet of sweet peas given him by a peculiar cleaning woman whom he meets at a streetcar stop. Unlike the cleaning woman who professes to hate the non-utilitarian flowers, the sergeant can appreciate them for their esthetic and romantic value, and he gives them to his wife who arranges them in a vase. The flowers become at the climax of the story the catalyst which sets off the sergeant's speculative mood, the rain in his heart. The bride herself is of course the chief symbol of the values the drill sergeant has been taught to love and respect. At the camp the sergeant wistfully recalls the image of "her soft, Southern voice, her small hands forever clasping a handkerchief"; but, when he actually sees her again, he finds her voice softer, her appearance fairer than he had remembered. Between them there is "complete understanding and sympathy," so much so that her qualities are brought to mind even when the sergeant sees his own face in a mirror.

The apartment which the bride has found is a retreat from the vulgar world of the army camp. As the sergeant rides toward it on the bus, he ponders the values of home and family:

> The sergeant was standing in the aisle but he bent over now and again and looked out of the windows at the neat bungalows and larger dwelling houses along the roadside. He would one day have a house such as one of these for his own. His own father's house was the like of these, with a screened porch on the side and a fine tile roof. He could hear his father saying, "A house is only as good as the roof over it." But weren't these the things that had once seemed prosaic and too binding for his notions? Before he went into the army had there not been moments when the thought of limiting himself to a genteel suburban life seemed intolerable by its restrictions and confinement? . . . And yet now when he sometimes lay wakeful and lonesome at night in the long dark barrack among the carefree and garrulous soldiers or when he was kneed and elbowed by the worried and weary mill hands on a bus, he dreamed longingly of the warm companionship he would find with her and their sober neighbors in a house with a fine roof. (75)

The apartment is in an "older" house with "old-fashioned" features, but it has at least one piece of furniture "they might have chosen themselves"; and, because the bride waits there, it becomes a pleasant haven for him.

Opposing the values of order, taste, and decorum which are represented by the bride and the apartment are the soldiers at the camp and the woman at the bus stop. The soldiers are quickly characterized by the bawdy banter they toss at the drill sergeant in the shower and barracks room as he prepares to leave on his overnight pass. After listening to their "stale, friendly, evil jokes," the sergeant thinks: "How unreal to him were these soldiers and their hairy bodies and all their talk and their rough ways. How temporary. How different from his own life, from his real life with her." Their vulgarity, amorality, and rootlessness all seem apparent in their dialogue. But later, when the sergeant is getting ready for bed in the apartment, he recalls the ugly remarks and reflects anew on their significance. "Their crudeness, their hardness, even their baseness—qualities that seemed to be taking root in the very hearts of those men—kept passing like objects through his mind," Taylor tells us.

An even more graphic impression is made by the cleaning woman the sergeant meets at the streetcar stop. She, too, is presented with imagery suggesting a slightly subhuman state:

> Her flat-chested and generally ill-shaped figure was clothed with a bag-like gingham dress that hung at an uneven knee-length. On her feet was a pair of flat-heeled brown oxfords. She wore white, ankle-length socks that emphasized the hairiness of her muscular legs. On her head a dark felt hat was drawn down almost to her eyebrows. Her hair was straight and of a dark color less rich than brown and yet more brown than black, and it was cut so that a straight not wholly greaseless strand hung over each cheek and turned upward just the slightest bit at the ends. (76)

Moreover, she is awkward in the presence of a simple natural beauty, holding her bouquet of sweet peas "as though they were a bunch of mustard greens" or "as a small boy holds flowers, half ashamed to be seen holding anything so delicate." She disclaims any appreciation for the flowers, professes in fact to hate them, and finally persuades the sergeant to take them from her. Then she engages the sergeant in a strained one-sided conversation, revealing an ugly puritan-like repression of sex and sensuality that contrasts with the easy self-indulgence of the soldiers. Reflecting later, the sergeant feels that the woman's "bitterness" is the quality which most presses upon him.

All of these things—the symbols of traditional values and of present experiences—bring the sergeant to a point of philosophical realization as he lies in bed beside his young wife. He has been thinking of the Civil War battle once fought in this area, of the sweet peas his wife has placed in a vase, and of his wife's perception and understanding; but his thoughts are interrupted by a rumbling streetcar.

> And before he could even speak the thoughts which he had been thinking, all those things no longer seemed to matter. The noise of the streetcar, the irregular rumble and uncertain clanging,

> brought back to him once more all the incidents of the day. He and his wife were here beside each other, but suddenly he was hopelessly distracted by this new sensation. The streetcar had moved away now beyond his hearing, and he could visualize it casting its diffused light among the dark foliage and over the white gravel between the tracks. He was left with the sense that no moment in his life had any relation to another. It was as though he were living a thousand lives. And the happiness and completeness of his marriage could not seem so large a thing. (86-87)

He is, in fact, able to clasp his bride in his arms again only when the rain begins once more outside: the rain which has made them seem "even more alone" in their newlyweds' apartment, the rain which sets them off like the "pleasing isolated arrangement of objects" his bride had made on the table in the living room.

V *"The Fancy Woman"*

It is appropriate that the sergeant in "Rain in the Heart" should come to reckon with his values when he leaves the all-male world of the army camp and travels to his bride's apartment. Peter Taylor is well aware that women can be demons who destroy or tutelary spirits who preside over and protect the value systems of any cultural group, and a final pair of stories in *A Long Fourth* provides a contrast between the two principal types of woman: woman as Lilith in "The Fancy Woman" and woman as Eve in "A Long Fourth."

"The Fancy Woman," the most frequently anthologized and and consequently probably the best known of all Taylor's stories, is in characterizations and point of view a very untypical sample of his work; but it is thematically closely related to the rest of his fiction. The central character, who provides the point of view for the whole story, is the "fancy woman" of the title: a Memphis trollop temporarily uprooted and uncomfortably transplanted onto the country estate of a wealthy lothario. During her brief pastoral adventure, the tarnished nymph Josie feels herself alternately humiliated and petted by her erstwhile lover George, patronized and mocked by his Negro servants and his guests from the city, and finally solicited and snubbed by his sons.

For Josie, the tensions of her new situation are oppressive; she has an almost paranoid sensitivity to the opinions of the supercilious strangers she confronts, but she lacks the fervor to counter them effectively. Josie is the kind of person who sizes up all other persons in terms of contrast to herself. She is very much aware that she is white and the servants she believes to be spying on her are black, that she is a woman and the visitors from Memphis are men, that she is youngish and the visitors' wives are aging, that she comes from one background and all these new people from another.

The contrasts which she feels are even more intensely painful where they involve her relationship with George and his two sons. The class difference provides the most obvious contrast; Josie is sure that George deliberately uses bad table manners and spices his conversation with Negroisms just to insult her. More important, however, is still another difference which one of the central images of the story brings out. To Josie, who has unpleasant memories of working in department stores, George in his meaner moods appears "no different from a floorwalker." A floorwalker, we come to realize, is in Josie's imagination the epitome of the exploiting class of mankind: the kind who get a "hold" on others and use them dispassionately for their own ends. And George, with more education, more money, more sense, but no more manners, is the floorwalker par excellence, who treats her "just like the floorwalker at Jobe's had that last week she was there," showing "no remorse, no compassion, and no humor" as he systematically degrades her.

As Josie begins to see George in this light, she resolves to turn the tables:

> She had had her fill of him and everybody else and was going to look out for her own little sweet self from now on.
>
> That was her trouble, she knew. She'd never made a good thing of people. "That's why things are like they are now," she said. "I've never made a good thing out of anybody." But it was real lucky that she realized it now, just exactly when she had, for it was certain that there had never been one whom more could be made out of than George. (38)

Her envisioned strategy is to find out what is wrong inside George ("for there's something wrong inside everybody") and to get "a hold on him" somehow. Josie thinks she sees the chance she wants when unexpected visitors drive out from Memphis: "'Guests,' he said, raising his eyebrows. And Josie felt that in that moment she had seen the strongest floorwalker weaken. George had scorned and laughed at everybody and every situation. But now he was ashamed. He was ashamed of her. On her behavior would depend his comfort. She was cold sober and would be *up* to whatever showed itself. It was her real opportunity" (42).

Surprised to find that the wives of George's friends are "old and plump" (and by analogy that George's own estranged wife must be oldish too), Josie thinks she has the upper hand. "George was the great floorwalker whose wife was old and who had shown his pride to Josie Carlson. He had shown his shame. Finally he had decided on a course and was following it, but he had given 'way his sore spots." As Josie ascends the stair with the three society matrons, believing that George is counting on her not to give herself away, she imagines that she is "soaring" upward into "the beginning of a new life" in which she might become "one of them"—one of the neatly corseted matrons with "lovely profiles and soft skin and natural-colored hair," one of George's own kind. The dream is shattered, however, as Josie, tiptoeing down the stairs, hears George and his men friends engaged in bawdy banter about her. "The girls are gonna be decent to her," she hears them say. "They agreed in the yard." Hearing, too, that George's teenage sons are coming the next day, Josie feels that she is "descending . . . once more into her old world": "He'll slick me some way if he has to for his kids, I think."

Josie is not immediately aware that her prime opportunity lies with the sons, not with the society guests. After an evening of drunken dancing and none-too-subtle flirtation, Josie even winds up sleeping with one of the guests. This incident is a psychological turning point for Josie, complete with moral revelation:

> "They're none of 'em any better than the niggers, I knew they couldn't be. Nobody is. By God, nobody's better than I am. Nobody can say anything to me." Everyone would like to live as free as she did! There was no such thing as . . . There was no such thing as what the niggers and the whites liked to pretend they were. She was going to let up, and do things in secret. Try to look like an angel. It wouldn't be as hard since there was no such thing. (48)

The next day, Josie meets George's sons—Jock, seventeen; Buddy, fourteen—who look "like two of those lovely wax models in the boy's department at Jobe's." Convinced now that even the supposedly innocent have smutty souls, Josie is humiliated when Buddy, reciting verses from Swinburne's "A Match" to the lady guests, chooses for her the one with the lines: "If you were queen of pleasure/And I were king of pain . . ." Later, during the night, she suspects that one of the boys is even trying to enter her bedroom through a bath that adjoins their room and hers.

The situation is now ripe for a melodramatic denouement in which the poor mistreated strumpet can seduce the son and wreak revenge on her sadistic oppressor. Taylor has, indeed, skillfully suggested such a possibility. George's Achilles' heel has already been foreshadowed for the reader in the very first paragraph of the story in a casual allusion to the two half-grown sons he is "so mortally fond of," a phrase repeated at the point where Josie discovers one of the sons has "notions." Furthermore, George has been described as gazing at his boys "like a floorwalker charmed by his wax manikins which had come to life." When George sends the elder son back to town, but inadvertently leaves Buddy alone in the house with Josie, the sentimental climax seems inevitable.

Peter Taylor is much too serious an artist, however, to provide so facile a conclusion to a complex story. When Buddy asks Josie, "Don't you think it's time you did something nice for me?" and requests her to pose for him; and, when Josie assumes he means for her to pose in the nude as a preliminary to something further, Taylor has Buddy unexpectedly reject Josie's inference: " 'That's not what I mean,' she heard the kid say again, without blinking an eye, without blushing. 'I didn't know you were that sort of nasty thing here. I didn't believe you were a fancy woman. Go on out of here. Go away!' he ordered her" (57-58). Josie, then, instead of triumphing over the hypocritical world around her the way romanticized demimondes traditionally do, descends the stairs once more in dejection. She is left to wait the angry displeasure of George, "wondering what he'd do to her."

The conclusion of "The Fancy Woman" is thus right for the purpose of both realistic characterization and thematic development. As Josie has revealed herself from the first scene on, she has emerged consistently as a weak, foolish, and irresolute woman who indulges in dream victories over her enemies, real and imagined (witness her dream conquest of the Negro servant, Amelia, and her fantasy of becoming good friends with one of the society matrons), but who can never take the first step in executing any plan of action (for instance, giving up the liquor which is her frequent undoing). She is, indeed, a "fancy woman," in more than one sense; for she lives in a world of imagination and her wishes are illusionary.

The chief insight of the story is also dependent upon the unromantic reversal at the end of the action. For Taylor does not believe Josie is right in her assumption that there is "no such thing" as the codes of values which others aspire to live by. Without any evidence beyond her own preconceptions, Josie has convinced herself that the Negro servants must be "all dosed up" because of promiscuity like her own, that the scar on Amelia's wrist must be a knife slash inflicted by the man-servant Henry (who "probably had raped his own children, the way niggers do"), that the cook Mammy steals food and has "likely killed enough niggers in her time to fill Jobe's basement." The same presuppositions apply to the white visitors, who she suspects will reveal their "true colors" and not act any better than she does "after they've got a few under their belts."

The damage Buddy does to her final hypothesis that "nobody's as damn smutty as a smart-alacky shaver" puts a new light on her basic judgment that "Everyone would like to live as free as she did." It is not that Josie has necessarily misjudged everyone; there is positive proof that some she meets (the guest who winds up in bed with her, for instance) are no better than she pictures them. Taylor does not even rule out the possibility that Jock and Buddy did have the very "notions" Josie suspected. The point is simply that Buddy did reject Josie and that he did so on moral grounds. Though there are hypocrites enough in the world, just as Josie deems, the world is not totally hypocritical; it is the overextension of the generalization that leads to Josie's error. Freedom from values and moral codes is not the desired lot of all mankind; and Josie, the "queen of pleasure," must be ever paired with the "king of pain," the sadist-lover who steps outside his own code to use the queen of pleasure and then contemptuously punishes her for her own amoral compliance.

The "fancy woman" is, in short, a failure. Setting herself apart from woman's hereditary role, Josie is an artificial substitute for what woman ought to be; she herself cannot tell the real from the imitation. When Josie admires an old vine-filled bucket which seems to go with the brick cistern that forms the base of the quaint breakfast table, Amelia sets her straight in words which apply not just to the bucket but to Josie as well: " 'No'm,' Amelia said . . .'They brung that out f'om Memphis and put it there like it was it.' "

VI *"The Real Tennessee Version"*

In the last story of his first volume, the story which gives the title to the book, Peter Taylor shows that the real and legitimate mistress of a house also has her problems. Harriet Wilson of "A Long Fourth" becomes, in fact, the thematic opposite of Josie Carlson in "The Fancy Woman." As conventional as Josie is unconventional, Harriet, a plump and pretty matron just past fifty, has no desire for the freedom Josie delights in. Her life is ruled by maxims from three respected sources of authority upon which women of her type have traditionally relied: mother, husband, and son. If Harriet has any uneasiness in accepting the guidance of these authorities, it is only when the instruction of the first two, which gives her comfort, conflicts with the instruction of the last, which sometimes disturbs her.

Though brilliantly individuated and more fully realized than perhaps any other character in Taylor's first book, Harriet is quickly seen to have symbolic significance as a latter-day hearth goddess, a custodian of domestic virtues and values. Living in an "old-fashioned" house, tending in her housekeeping to rigidity and an overdone care for "cleanliness and order," maintaining an expert interest in matters of genealogy and kinship, holding romantic attachments to the home environment, and loving inordinately "the old songs that were fixed so well in her ear and in her heart," Harriet is almost the archetypal mother. Like the version of the ballad "Barbara Allen" which she sings, she is authentic—"the real Tennessee version" of what she stands for.

Harriet's firm grounding in a particular cultural reality is, however, part of her limitation. She is unable to recognize herself in others destined to play the same maternal role. Specifically, she fails to see any parallel between herself and her old Negro servant Mattie or, later and less importantly, between herself and

Ann Prewitt, the girl her son brings home on a visit. The conflicts within Harriet develop when old Mattie points out the similarity in their two situations. On this Fourth of July weekend in a year during World War II, apparently 1943, Harriet is awaiting a farewell visit from her son before he goes into the army when Mattie learns that her nephew BT, whom she has raised as a foster son, must go to work at "th'air fact'ry" to avoid being drafted. "It's like you losin' Mr. Son," Mattie says of her own plight, sending Harriet into paroxysms of indignation at the comparison. Harriet, who despite a patronizing affection for the Negro woman firmly adheres to her husband's maxim that "we can't judge Negroes the way we do white people," is apparently appalled by the suggested similarity between her own dear son and Mattie's odoriferous nephew. Subconsciously, however, Harriet is probably reacting primarily to the identification of herself and Mattie in the same role.

The details of the story suggest that the identification Mattie makes is more pertinent than Harriet realizes. Both Harriet and Mattie represent values their "sons" have repudiated. Son, Harriet's boy—despite his reputation as a "model son" who is faithful and considerate to his parents, not grieving them "with youthful dissipation as most Nashville boys do"—nevertheless has "advanced ideas" which seem "peculiar" and "radical" to the people of Nashville; and he writes "disturbing articles" in national magazines. And BT, though "acknowledged a good hand at many services which could be rendered on the back porch" in the open air, lacks the qualities white people like Harriet find attractive in his Aunt Mattie and other Negroes: "He had neither good manners nor the affectionate nature nor the appealing humor that so many niggers have." Neither Son nor BT follows traditional moral codes; the intellectual Son does not believe in marriage, and BT brings black "female-things" from Nashville to his shack. Furthermore, both are about to be lost to their "mothers" because of forces larger than the individuals involved—the distant but destructive war.

Son's holiday homecoming finally leads Harriet to a new self-awareness. The catalyst is found in Harriet's spitefully spinsterish daughters, Kate and Helena, who set out on a deliberate campaign to embarrass Son and his "Platonic" girl friend, Ann Prewitt, by aping cloyingly the qualities of Southern womanhood which Harriet takes seriously. When Harriet hears them mincing out "the very reverse of ideas they usually expressed" (including the etiquette of Harriet's mother and the philosophy of the Vanderbilt Agrarians) and pretending allegiance to "the customs and ways that used to pertain in Nashville," she is at first pleased; but she finally realizes they are maliciously parodying all that is conventional in her way of life.

Her shock is compounded when she learns that Son has apparently acted with the same sort of callous cruelty to his unconventional friend who has quite conventionally fallen in love with him. And Ann Prewitt, though she is the editor of a birth-control magazine and ostensibly an intellectual radical, is perhaps closer in her values to Harriet than any of Harriet's own children; she, at least, has an emotional center capable of sensitivity and love. "*Her* girls had never been in love," Harriet is made to realize at one point. "They're like Son, she thought, and it isn't in them."

Disappointed in her own maternal relationships (the moment in which Son would come to tell her "what is in his heart" never materializes), Harriet discovers that Mattie suffers too when BT brings one of his black "female-things" to the shack on his last night home. Sweetheart, Harriet's husband, insists that Harriet go to comfort Mattie, not understanding their estrangement and asking, "Harriet, why should this be so hard for you?"—a question which Harriet feels is "making a larger and more general inquiry into her character" than had ever been done before.[2] When Harriet does go and apologize to Mattie in BT's reeking shack, the scene is poignant:

> Mattie raised her eyes to her mistress, and there was neither forgiveness nor resentment in them. In her protruding lower lip and in her wide nostrils there was a defiance, but it was a defiance of the general nature of this world where she must pass her days, not of Harriet in particular. In her eyes there was grief and there was something beyond grief. After a moment she did speak, and she told Harriet that she was going to sit here all night and that they had all better go on to bed in the house. Later when Harriet tried to recall the exact tone and words Mattie had used—as her acute ear would normally have allowed her to do—she could not reconstruct the speech at all. It seemed as though Mattie had used a special language common to both of them but one they had never before discovered and could now never recover. (165-66)

Back in her room, Harriet tries successively to resume her broken prayers, to weep, and to comprehend her experience:

> She thought of all the talking that Son and the girls had done and she felt that she was even beginning to understand what it had meant. But she sadly reflected that her children believed neither what Ann Prewitt nor what the professors at the University were offering them. To Harriet it seemed that her children no longer existed; it was as though they had all died in childhood as people's children used to do. All the while she kept remembering that Mattie was sitting out in that shack for the sole purpose of inhaling the odor in the stifling air of BT's room. (166)

The conflicts in "A Long Fourth," then, are not the apparent ones: the conflicts between generations with differing ideas, or between races with different colors. Harriet is not cut off from her children because they are radical and she is conservative and conventional, but because she holds some values and ideas, and they hold none. And the superficial estrangement, based on racial and social distinctions, between herself and Mattie is not a lasting one because the two women share something more fundamental in their common role of "mother."

Ann Prewitt has mentioned that Son has been reading Oswald Spengler's *Decline of the West,* and the allusion provides a clue to a possible interpretation of the story. The whole situation can almost be seen as a microcosm demonstrating Spengler's cultural theories. The living Southern "Culture" (preserving the fundamentals of the Western heritage) represented by Harriet is being succeeded by the declining "Civilization" stage represented by her children, especially Son. Harriet, Mattie, and Ann all are variations on Spengler's concept of woman: standing close to the Cosmic, rooted deep in the earth, immediately "involved in the grand cyclic rhythms of Nature," actually being (rather than experiencing, making, or comprehending) Destiny, History, Time. For woman, Spengler says, history is a "cosmic flow," "*the cultureless history of the generation-sequence,* which never alters, but uniformly and stilly passes through the being of all animal and human species, through all the short-lived individual Culttures," whereas for man history is "political, social, more conscious, freer, and more agitated than the other."[3] Spengler argues:

> Here, in man and in woman, *the two kinds of History* are fighting for power. Woman is strong and wholly what she is, and she experiences the Man and the Sons only in relation to herself and her ordained role. In the masculine being, on the contrary, there is a certain contradiction; he is the man, and he is something else besides, which woman neither understands nor admits, which she feels as robbery and violence upon that which to her is holiest. . . .
>
> And so woman despises that other History—man's politics—which she never comprehends, and of which all that she sees is that it takes her sons from her. . . . Man's history sacrifices woman's history to itself, . . . but nevertheless there was and is and ever will be a secret politic of the woman—of the female of the animal world even—that seeks to draw away her male from his kind of history and to weave his body and soul into her own plantlike history of generic succession—that is, unto herself. . . .
>
> Thus, history has two meanings, neither to be blasphemed. It is cosmic or politic, it *is* being or it *preserves* being. There are two sorts of Destiny, two sorts of war, two sorts of tragedy—*public and private*. . . . The double significance of directional Time finds its highest expression in the ideas of *the State* and *the Family*.[4]

In Spengler's theory of the organic life cycle of cultures, fertility belongs to the Culture stage and sterility to the Civilization stage. "The primary woman, the peasant woman, is *mother*," Spengler says; and Taylor has made Harriet a real mother and Mattie an equally committed foster mother. "But now emerges the Ibsen woman, the comrade, the heroine of a whole megalopolitan literature from Northern drama to Parisian novel," Spengler adds. "Instead of children, she has soul-conflicts; marriage is craft-art for the achievement of 'mutual understanding.' "[5] And Taylor gives us Ann Prewitt, the birth-control proponent, the Platonic mistress, the woman with soul-conflicts and no children.

Is Taylor arguing that Western culture, or at least its manifestation in the southern United States, has (to use Spengler's seasonal metaphor) passed its fecund summer? In the last line of the story, Taylor writes: "When she opened her eyes it was dark and there was the chill of autumn night about the room." The inference is possible (especially when we recall that Harriet has just noted that her children seemed no longer to exist, to have died in childhood); but there is no compulsion to make it. Even without the Spenglerian analogies, "A Long Fourth" is on its most literal level a subtle enough story about the complexities of cultural values—old and new, male and female, black and white. As the final story of a volume that began with "The Soutmaster," its simple and sufficient point may be that the young men from all over the nation have not yet demanded—as Uncle Jake hoped they might demand someday—"a return to the old ways and the old teachings everywhere."

CHAPTER 3

A Woman of Means

I *The Short Story Writer's "Trap"*

A *LONG FOURTH*, although well-received by the reviewers, met the fate of most first short-story collections: neglect by the book-buying public. It was perhaps inevitable, then, that Peter Taylor would fall into what Katherine Anne Porter has called the "trap" every short-story writer must beware of.[1] That trap is, of course, the novel, the one literary form with some likelihood of showing a profit in the bookstores. *A Woman of Means,*[2] Peter Taylor's first and only novel is, however, a novel only by a rather generous extension of the term. It is, in the first place, just a little more than thirty thousand words in length. It has only a small cast of characters, almost no plot, a carefully controlled tonal unity, and none of the large-scale fictional fireworks usually expected of the modern novel. Furthermore, two hefty sections of it were published previously as short stories in the *New Yorker* and *Harper's Bazaar.*[3] In a way, it is only the magnification of Taylor's short-story methods to a slightly larger scale; and it thus provides a good basis for an examination of Taylor's characteristic techniques.

What kind of work is Taylor's first full-length effort? It is, as might be expected from the short stories which preceded it, another retrospective first-person narrative about urban family life. Specifically, it is an account of an adolescent boy's complex relationship with a wealthy and doting stepmother and of the stepmother's neurotic disintegration. The narrator is Quintus Cincinnatus Lovell Dudley, whose improbable name, as a reflection of his Southern heritage, is one key to the role he plays. Quint is a half-orphan whose mother died at his birth and left him to be reared by his father alone. But Quint's father, Gerald Dudley, is a traveling hardware salesman, and being raised by him meant moving from boarding house to boarding house and transferring from school to school in town after town. Quint's description of the year he and his father were living in Louisville provides a glimpse of his childhood environment:

> We lived in a good boarding house there, better than any place we had lived in before, and we each had a big room with a double bed. We had a private bathroom with a tile shower, and we had a little porch of our own. A Negro maid served us breakfast in our rooms; we ate dinner in the big restaurants and cafeterias downtown. Twice that winter Father took me to St. Louis, where I met the president and several vice-presidents of the hardware company, and I remember the president's taking me aside to tell me that that father of mine had a real head on his shoulders, a real drive about him and good business sense. On the first trip we stayed at the Chase Hotel. I spent most of the days in our room, gazing out the window or sailing paper arrows out over Lindell Boulevard toward Forest Park. . . .
>
> That winter in Louisville Father took me to several picture shows. Neither of us had seen many motion pictures before this, and when we came back to the boarding house after a show, Father seemed always excited and full of talk. If the movie was about poor people he would talk of the days when he had first left the farm. If it was about rich people he would talk of the friends he had made in St. Louis and say that in a few years he and I would *have things* and *be somebody* ourselves. (22-23)

During the summers, Quint was usually sent to Belgrove, his maternal grandmother's farm in Tennessee. Grandma Lovell's place is nothing pretentious: it has a privy down by the chicken yard, a greenhouse and an old tobacco barn, a springhouse where the little Negro boys love to wade when the door's not locked, a porch where uncles and aunts can visit, and broad lawns where Quint and his country cousins can play. It is, from one point of view, "a run-down farm" belonging to "a poor-little-old country woman," as Quint's father sometimes describes it. But it also has romantic souvenirs of another day: a lone white oak and a solitary magnolia, an old abandoned formal garden with broken urns and untrimmed hedges, a cannon on the lawn and a stack of rusty shells on the ell porch, the grass-covered mounds of an Indian graveyard, and nearby trenches where Confederate soldiers had died in the Battle of Nashville.

Quint's rural pursuits are severely limited, however, by the overprotective restrictions his father makes and insists that the grandmother enforce. Gerald Dudley will not let his son go barefooted for more than a minute; will not let him venture off with his cousins and the little Negroes on expeditions to Radnor Lake or Wild Man's Hill; will not, in fact, ever let him forget that he is "mostly a city boy, not on to country things like the others." And, though Quint in some ways seems to love the country, he comes to feel awkward and out of place there—eventually repudiating it altogether when, before the taunts of his city friends, he becomes ashamed of his grandfather's watch which his grandmother sends him for his twelfth birthday.

The first significant change in Quint's fortunes occurs when he is ten and his father is moved to St. Louis and begins a rapid rise in his company. Gerald Dudley in quick succession is made a vice-president, is invited to join a country club and a men's town club, and meets the wealthy and charming Anna Lauterbach, the woman of means of the title. Mrs. Lauterbach, the only daughter of a St. Louis millionaire and the ex-wife of the heir to a brewery fortune, is perhaps more attracted to the prospective son she envisions in Quint than to the prospective husband she sees in Gerald. At any rate, Gerald Dudley soon weds her; and he and Quint then move into the monstrous Italian palace Mrs. Lauterbach's father had built for her the year she had made her debut.

Life at Casa Anna is all novelty for Quint. He has two pretty teenage stepsisters to amuse him. He has servants to wait on him. He attends a country day school during the year and spends summers in Michigan at a resort. He is able to put down roots in a stable home environment. And, best of all, he finds a mother's love and solicitude lavished on him by his beautiful stepmother. Quint, with rare lyricism, recalls his feelings when he came into "practical possession of a mother":

> I thought of the peculiar happiness of loving her as I did, and I thought of the firmness with which I was established in her heart. Suddenly I had become the carefree hero of a wonderful adventure, and I was ready to have all the fun of it. It seemed that she had given me the power to breathe and that she was at the same time the breath and the air breathed. And just as it is not necessary to remember to breathe in the midst of a foot race, from that day forward mere thoughts about her would become too tedious for me to bother with. (81-82)

So self-confident does Quint become in his new situation that he is able to establish himself as best-all-round-boy in his division of the country day school and to win at the age of thirteen the coveted Dartmouth Cup on Class Day. But already the seeds of change have been planted. Personal conflicts begin to disrupt the idyllic menage. Gerald, who has by this time become president of his company, faces a showdown with the board of directors; and, disturbed by this incident, he is offended by a slight which he believes one of the stepdaughters shows him. He sulks off on a business trip and spoils a family holiday, not for the daughters, but for his wife and Quint. Gerald soon after proposes a South American vacation—as "amends," his wife believes—but cancels the plans when the board of directors fires him. Because the news of the cancellation is broken to her while she is trying on her travel trousseau for him, Anna feels she has been deliberately humiliated by her husband; and a bitter quarrel ensues. Anna's suspicion that Gerald has married her for her money—though he refuses to accept her offer to manage her financial affairs and, in fact, takes a non-executive sales position with another company—is renewed; so, too, is Gerald's suspicion that Anna married him for his son.

Highly distraught and fearing Gerald may try to take his son away, Anna begins to imagine herself pregnant and refuses to believe the doctors who deny that she is. Her neurotic withdrawal into fantasy is not revealed, however, until she becomes physically ill one day and blames the illness on the imagined pregnancy. Her prognosis is not good, and her daughters finally decide to send her away to a sanitarium in the East and to dispose of her mansion by dismantling it and selling the components at auction. On the same day that news of Lindbergh's "amazing solo flight" across the Atlantic is announced, Quint sees his stepmother led away to the institution while the rest of the family debates the question of "Who's to blame?"

II *"The Amazing Solo Flight"*

The basic story, then, of *A Woman of Means* is not very complicated. But the execution of the novel is, like Lindbergh's aeronautical feat, an "amazing solo flight." Sometimes one might wonder, even, how Peter Taylor got his lighter-than-air craft off the ground, to say nothing of how he got it to soar past some very rough currents to its final destination. The narrative course, for one thing, is not plotted on a linear chart. The novel opens with a scene of Quint's happy life in his stepmother's home: his memories of his stepsisters confiding secrets to their diaries, of his father reveling in the girls' joshing chatter over a billiards table, of his stepmother recalling incidents of her youth. But immediately we are shown Quint worrying about potential accidents which might spoil his blissful contentment, and the pathetic ending of the novel is already foreshadowed.

Quint's anxieties are linked to his past experiences in boarding-house life, which are unobtrusively introduced in casually reflective flashbacks. "I began to think that my father's wisdom and strength and good faith were almost superhuman," Quint says; "for our present household represented the faithful keeping of promises that he might very well not have been able to keep. Remembering those promises sometimes set me to thinking about the days when he had made them. I could remember . . ."—and he is off into a description of the contrast of earlier times.

For two and one half chapters of the four in the novel, the narration moves back and forth from the more remote past of Quint's early childhood to the happy days with his new mother; from the middle of the third chapter to the end of the novel, the action moves more straightforwardly to its climax, with only an occasional anticipation of a future event or a passing allusion to a past one. The method is nothing radical or experimental, nothing really innovative like, say, the "tunnelling process" Virginia Woolf discovered in writing *Mrs. Dalloway*. But the method is a particularly apt adaptation of what has almost become the conventional handling of time in the post-Jamesian novel.

What is perhaps more interesting in the structural technique is the surprising principle by which incidents in various periods of time are selected for dramatization. Many seemingly insignificant happenings are related in such detail that one expects latent significance: how will the girls' diaries figure in the plot? when will Miss Moore, the schoolteacher whom Quint's father dates briefly in St. Louis, figure in Quint's life again? what will the Dartmouth Cup come to symbolize? But these are questions which lead nowhere; to ask them is, in fact, to misread the novel. Such questions assume that details of character and action exist not for themselves but for something more abstract, such as "story," "theme," or "pre-conceived effect," as indeed they might in much modern fiction.

Peter Taylor, however, was not writing a piece of this sort in *A Woman of Means*. The compression and condensation of experience, so sought after by many of his artistic contemporaries, has never been his method; he is leisurely either by nature or by design. A fellow short-story writer, J. F. Powers, has well described Taylor's technique:

> If Taylor even remembers, he refuses to tell a story the way it was told before. He refuses, moreover, to exploit his material to the limit, to manufacture characters, drama, suspense—in short, he won't traffic in what is known as a "strong story line." He refuses to be electric. He knows that life itself has a very weak story line. To render it truly he distils it, though again not as you might think: his work is not remarkable for its form and conciseness. He likes to take a while to get a story underway.[4]

The very casualness of this approach is contributory to the verisimilitude of the novel: people and events seem to be in the novel not because they are intended to mean something but simply because they are part of its reality.

And the people are, as usual in Peter Taylor's fiction, what we remember best about *A Woman of Means*. Several highly complex characterizations emerge in the short length of the novelette. The crucial one, of course, is Quint's—for it is through his consciousness that the other characters are seen; and, if he is a failure, the others must be failures also. Quint, as a narrator, is no Holden Caulfield, no subjective adolescent still reacting to the experiences of an immediate past. He is rather, more like Melville's Wellingboro Redburn, a mature adult detachedly reflecting on a process of maturation that took place some time ago. He neither bullies his audience into a reluctant intimacy nor holds it off with a cold formality. He is merely the necessary intermediary for experience that somehow seems worth re-creating.

Kenneth Clay Cathey has felt that Taylor has not "synthesized well enough" Quint's story with the stepmother's. He has complained also that too much of the earlier part of the novel is taken up with "exposition of the boy's life before his father's remarriage, exposition which really adds nothing to the understanding of his eventual psychological change." Cathey calls this a defect in novelistic form, a failure to depict especially in the stepmother, but also in Quint "a moral *evolution* instead of the moral *revelation* which is central to the short story."[5] But Quint does evolve, and the stages of his evolution are rather clearly marked by several key scenes. The first is when his father tries to tell him a "dream" he had one night of marrying again, and Quint realizes suddenly that he has always hated his father's "business drive" and realizes simultaneously that he himself is "the very center and core of it." The second is when his father announces his engagement, and Quint realizes that all the decisions that the rich widow and her daughters and his father may make in the future will inevitably affect him, that he is bound up in involuntary interpersonal relationships. The third is when the headmaster identifies him as "Anna Lauterbach's boy" and leads Quint to the "practical possession of a mother" and a mother's love, to the voluntary acceptance of a binding relationship. The fourth in one sense reverses the direction of Quint's evolution, for it is when Quint wins the Dartmouth Cup and, annoyed and resentful of his stepmother's intrusion on the day of his personal triumph, asserts his independence by rejecting her silent demand to turn the cup over to her. And the final step in the evolution is Quint's beginning of his own Lindbergh-like solo flight on the day his stepmother is taken irrevocably away from him to the sanitarium. Quint has, in short, grown up through several important steps toward a mature independence.

The other characters are, of course, known to us only as Quint describes them, but their portraits are both credible and vivid. Grandmother Lovell, for instance, is a minor character whose function in the novel is minimal; but she emerges in sharply-etched lines in her few short scenes, especially in the one where she opposes Gerald's over-protectiveness of Quint. The physical images are sparse—we hear her talking "vaguely" of the values of country life, and we see her once retorting with her lips "suddenly drawn tight over her false teeth"—but the total impression of her inarticulate but implacable dignity is hardly dependent upon these. Though she must give in to Gerald's demands that she restrict Quint's activities, her unvanquished inner resources and values are made clear: "When he had driven away in the taxi, Grandma called me into the pantry and held my hand while she gave out the lunches she had packed for the cousins and for the two Negro children. They were leaving for a swimming expedition to Brown's Creek. One lunch, wrapped in brown oiled paper, was left on the pantry cupboard" (47).

So, too, the teenage stepsisters, Bess and Laura, are brought to life with a great economy of technique: by tags of slangy speech ("Pardon me, I've got to go tell Diary something rich"), by incidental mention of their interests (collecting pillows and china dogs, planning holiday parties at the country club), by arrested images against a background ("They had wrapped themselves in their velvet capes, their voices had sounded crisp and thrilling in the hall for a moment, and then the heavy front door had slammed"). They are pretty, silly, and vain, and hence fill a stereotype; but they are also individuals whose actions, believable in retrospect, are not necessarily predictable in advance. Their initial response to their mother's illness, for instance, is one of idealistic devotion: "When they had first arrived, they insisted that they would never under any circumstances consent to her commitment to any sort of institution. They busied themselves preparing her meals and attending her from morning till night." By the end of the second week, however, they have decided to send their mother off to a sanitarium in the East and to have her cherished house dismantled and sold in pieces; and Bess has gotten herself engaged to a band leader.

The most interesting of the secondary characters is Quint's father, who sometimes seems transparently shallow, sometimes darkly complex. Gerald Dudley is in many ways the typical self-made American bourgeois, with the typical virtues ("an air of innocence," stoic dignity, diligence, perseverance, straightforward honesty) and the typical faults ("too austere integrity," stubborn pride, over-zealous ambition, single-mindedness, preoccupation with success). Once, when Quint looks out a hotel window to see his father getting out of a taxi with two other businessmen, he thinks that he "could not have distinguished him from the other men on the sidewalk except for the old-fashioned broad-brimmed hat he wore." At another time, Quint gets goose bumps noticing how exactly his father's expression is like those in the pictures of company officers and directors on the wall of his office.

Gerald Dudley is individuated, however, because he manifests personal attitudes which spring from hidden sources within him and because he enters into kinds of relationships which defy easy categorization. One conversation with Quint is especially revealing of his inner feeling:

> He told me about the things he had learned when he was a farm boy himself and how it never helped him any to know those things when he went into business. "We had only a poor ridge farm," he said, "and we fought nature with nature. We always let the martins bin up in the eaves of our house to drive off the hawks. How they did use to scare me when they whizzed past my window upstairs at night. Our house was a real old timer with the eaves coming right down over the little square upstairs windows. There were no windows at all in the gables." He talked without sentiment, as though he were merely giving evidence. "There were always snakes in the corn crib to keep the rats away. And my daddy would never let us kill a skunk—not even the nasty one that had her kittens under our house one year—because he said they killed rats and kept away varmints. You learn a lot of things in the country, especially where there are no niggers around to get between you and the real work, but a mighty lot of good it did me when I went into hardware." (49)

Though the passage is at least partly ironical (learning to fight nature with nature has perhaps been part of Gerald's business success), it is also a credible literal explanation of his views. Gerald is capable of surprising us, too, by the delicate sensitivity of his affection for his stepdaughters, by his tender solicitude for his son, and by his stoic dignity in rising resiliently from his failure in business. The most convincing proof, moreover, that Peter Taylor has not oversimplified this character lies in the fact that we can never answer with absolute certainty the question which the stepmother raises: did he really marry her only for her money? The evidence, even when carefully weighed and sifted, can tip the balance either way.

III "*A Spoiled Rich Woman*"

Those who have found *A Woman of Means* disappointing have usually laid the blame to the characterization of the title character. Surely, Anna Lauterbach is the most intriguing and the most mysterious of all the personalities encountered in the book. She is in outward appearances beautiful, charming, talented, witty, gay, poised, contented—the farthest thing from the "corpulent little woman dressed in black" with pockmarked face, kinky bob, freckled arms, and stubby fingers loaded with diamonds whom Quint visualizes when first hearing of her. Inside, however, she is a bundle of frustrations and anxieties which finally produce the mental breakdown at the end of the novel. The artistic question is whether this denouement is sufficiently prepared for.

A careful reading of the details presented shows that Taylor has sprung no O. Henry-type surprises but has released forces which merely reach a natural, if not wholly foreseen, conclusion. Besides symbolic foreshadowing (Quint's morbid fear of a fatal accident in the family, for instance), Taylor gives ample clues that the stepmother's interior life is not so healthy as it might be. The first hint lies in the unusually strong attachment to her husband's son—an attachment so strong that Gerald Dudley has even accused her of marrying him just to get Quint. Whatever repressed sexual impulses may lie behind this attachment are only suggested, not exploited, by the author; and the relationship is open to interpretation on other levels. The second hint about Anna Lauterbach's inner state comes from the passages where she discusses her wealth and the paradoxical sense of insecurity which it has created in her. Her consciousness of her wealth came only when her schoolmates in Switzerland forced it; "I had never thought of our being so rich before we left St. Louis and went to Europe," she tells Quint. But the schoolmates' constant behind-the-back reference to her as "the American millionairess" built up a suspiciousness within her: "it seemed that that was all in me that interested them: my money" and "whenever I was about to invite some girl [as a companion on a holiday trip], she always said something that made me think she didn't like me for myself."

Anna Lauterbach's desire for a son, then, is at least partially a desire for someone who will love her for herself, the way her own father loved her when he built Casa Anna for her. She does not find this kind of love in her first marriage to the brewery heir (whom she treats like a little boy) or even in her second marriage to Gerald Dudley. She thinks she has found it in Quint until his burgeoning desire for adult independence asserts itself. And this disappointment brings her final mental collapse; having failed to attain her desires in reality, she turns to fantasy and imagines herself to be carrying in her womb the son who will love her for herself. At the climax of the novel, then, she repeats the old accusation once more, this time to Quint: "You deceitful little wretch," she cries to him, "you're plotting with the rest of them to smother my baby! And *you*'re after my money, too!" It is not so much the hysterical pregnancy as this final rejection of reality which marks her complete psychological disintegration.

All of the characterizations in *A Woman of Means* have several features in common. In the first place, none of them is simply a stereotype, though each bears some obvious traits of a character type. But Anna Lauterbach cannot be explained with the easy label "spoiled rich woman" which Gerald pins on her in a quarrel, anymore than Gerald can be adequately explained as an American bourgeois or Bess and Laura as fickle teenagers. Furthermore, the characters do not fall into neat moral categories: there are no heroes or villains in this novel. Not a single character is completely unsympathetic and not a single character is without moral flaws.

Nor are the characters mere representatives or emblems of other things, without interest in themselves, with importance only in their symbolic frame. Though Peter Taylor's characters do often suggest something more than what they literally are, they are in this novel, as elsewhere, of primary importance as people truthfully re-created. The secret of their lasting attraction lies in the reality of their complicated interrelationships. They are, in fact, known and defined precisely by their interactions with other characters and with their environment.

Here Peter Taylor's style serves its important function. For it is a style which communicates with sensitivity the nuances of personal relationships. It is not the kind of style which hovers over external reality like a determined hummingbird sipping out the last drop of nectar. Matter-of-fact reality is presented matter of factly without stylistic grace notes. If Peter Taylor wishes to communicate the sense of bigness Quint feels in the new school where he enrolls, he makes Quint say, "It was the biggest school I had ever seen." If he wishes to describe a twilight scene, he straightforwardly writes, "It was late but it was still quite sunny." Yet this same simple style can do yeoman's work in clarifying subtle personal relationships, as in this example where Quint's parents become aware he has been listening to an adult conversation:

> My father glanced warily at me and all of a sudden became preoccupied with two sailboats out on the lake. His wife with equal suddenness gave way to irrepressible and infectious laughter. "Do you think, Gerald," she said, "that our boy here misses a single trick?" Then looking at me she spoke in an alto voice that I recognized as imitative of my own. "Anyhow, he probably knows twice as much as his old man." I tried to give a knowing look, because I thought it was expected of me. Then I saw my father turn his blue eyes from the lake to her with a smile that was submissive. At such moments it seemed that she meant to him exactly what she meant to me, and that without her we might now be sitting together on the porch of some summer hotel looking dumbly at the strangers about us. It was mid-morning, and springing up in a burst of energy, I challenged my father to a swim in the lake. (61-62)

It is in this kind of passage, too, that the rare figurativeness in Taylor's style makes its appearance. The figure is, as likely as not, used to pinpoint a relationship, as "I felt that I was looking at both Father and Mother through the wrong end of Mother's opera glasses," or, "Her eyes appeared to have been circled with gray crayon, and from their depths she peered at me as though I were a blinding beam of light."

Despite its simplicity, the Taylor style in *A Woman of Means* is literate, urbane, and intelligent. Though the sensitivity of the adolescent Quint is at the center of the book, there is no effort to write Salingerese imitations of adolescent style. The book fits what the linguist Martin Joos has labeled the "consultative" variety of language usage: the variety most used in ordinary human relationships, not so deliberative as the "formal" and "frozen" styles, not so informal as the "casual" or the "intimate."[6] It has thus the colloquial quality appropriate to the first-person narration, or at least it gives the illusion of having it. Malcolm Cowley has noted that in the best Southern fiction one seems to hear "the voice of the narrator talking, rather than the sound of his typewriter clacking,"[7] and Peter Taylor's voice is one of those that emerges most distinctly.

IV *On Its Own Terms*

Because the Taylor style in *A Woman of Means* (as, indeed, in most of his other works) suggests a conversational approach, it presents the subject with an anecdotal objectivity that seldom makes explicit its thematic significance. "This is how it was," Taylor seems to say, not "This is what it means." As a result, the reader of *A Woman of Means,* however satisfying he may have found the novelette as a vicarious experience, may find it difficult to pinpoint and paraphrase its insights into life. It is undoubtedly easier to say what the book is not than what it is.

Of the several types of book which it might have been, *A Woman of Means* is most emphatically not a naturalistic account of bourgeois manners and morals. Though it is firmly grounded in realistic detail, verifiable by any observer of American life, the novel never relies on the uncritical amassing of mere facts to achieve its effect; rather, it creates the impression that an evaluative intelligence has economically and purposefully directed the selection of details. The subject matter may be the most intimate of family situations, but the treatment lacks the *voyeur*istic emphasis on the sordid side of sex which has come to characterize the naturalistic novel. Anna Lauterbach may in some externals resemble the heroines of John O'Hara, but she is a fictional creation of an entirely different order.

If it is not naturalistic, neither is the novel clinical. Though the Phaedra theme might have invited more of the amateur psychoanalysis so prevalent in modern fiction, Taylor forgoes the temptation. Obviously Anna's obsessive predilection for her stepson suggests psychological problems, perhaps erotic in origin. Her relationships to her father, to her first husband, and to Quint's father indicate her failure to mature in some crucial aspects of her personality. And certainly her hysterical pregnancy, her developing paranoia, and her eventual mental deterioration could be greatly elucidated by Freudian theories. Still, Taylor's interest in Anna is not psychiatric; he nowhere gives the impression of attempting a clinical study of a neurotic's psychological disintegration.

The sociological is of even less concern than the psychological. Despite a clear-cut class contrast among his principal characters, Taylor does not exploit the possibilities for social satire. Gerald Dudley, we have already seen, shares many qualities of the typical opportunistic American businessman; but he never becomes a Babbitt-like caricature. Anna Lauterbach is the pampered heiress, but she is neither blamed nor ridiculed by the author for her condition. The snobbery which Quint confronts at the country day school to which his wealthy stepmother sends him is presented dispassionately as an objective fact with little or no comment, either explicit or implicit. Even the semi-comic attempts of a character from one social situation to adjust to a different one (witness Gerald's embarrassment on his concert date with the St. Louis schoolteacher or Quint's awkwardness on his Grandmother Lovell's farm) are treated as matters of personal characterization rather than as occasions for social satire. This is not to say that Taylor's gentle irony does not pervade every social situation in the novel, only that it never takes a central importance.

Unlike many other novels by contemporary Southerners, *A Woman of Means* also avoids historical allegory. It is a fact pertinent to the total implications of the story, of course, that Gerald and Quint come from rural Tennessee while Anna Lauterbach is a daughter of metropolitan Missouri. It is also not insignificant that Anna wins Quint away from his Grandmother Lovell, who would have given him an entirely different kind of upbringing. Taylor might have made his novel a parable recounting the old-fashioned South's loss of its sons to the progressive Midwest, the replacement of the agrarian ideal by the urban-industrial fact, or the wooing and unfortunate wedding of outside capital by New South opportunism. The novel is, indeed, susceptible in some degree to each of these semi-allegorical interpretations; but whatever meanings accrue to the story in this area provide overtones but not the major harmonics.

Finally, this story of a youth's awakening avoids also the pitfalls of the sentimental Bildungsroman which are such a peril to so many young fiction writers who are producing their first novels. It is only retrospectively, in fact, that the reader becomes fully aware that this is primarily Quint's story and that the pattern has followed closely the pattern of many another novel of adolescent experiences. Perhaps because Quint is younger and less self-conscious than most Bildungsroman heroes, perhaps because he shares the stage with the more dramatic character of his stepmother, perhaps because Taylor's delicate irony is ever at work and his style is ever spare and wary of excess, *A Woman of Means* escapes the romantic subjectivity that has been the ruin of so many of its prototypes.

If Peter Taylor has written neither a naturalistic document nor a clinical study nor a sociological diatribe nor a historical allegory nor a sentimental Bildungsroman, what has he written? The answer is simple but evasive: he has written a novel which, like all good works of art, can be fully comprehended only on its own individual terms, not in the generic terms of a literary type. Though *A Woman of Means* has affinities with each of the types mentioned, it emerges finally as a composite form. Like all novels, it deals with human interrelationships; but it does not clearly focus on any single aspect of the interrelationships the way the more readily classifiable works of fiction tend to do. Instead, it reveals human experience through a selection of realistic details of many different sorts fused together to give the illusion of life met directly in all its complexity without the benefit of artistic simplification and interpretation. Hence, the apparent thematic ambiguity of it: we may find ourselves as reluctant to try to "explain" this vicarious experience as we would be to explain a real-life set of events. The very satisfaction we feel at the completion of the story, however, suggests that the experience has been crystallized for us in an artistic form which it would not have in real life. In short, we know we have responded to patterns of plot, character development, image, and verbal presentation which condition our reaction and prescribe the boundaries of meaning.[8]

Despite its failure to present a readily paraphrasable theme and to fit into one of the usual categories, *A Woman of Means* is certainly the best known and perhaps the most widely praised of Peter Taylor's works. Drawing generally good reviews everywhere, it received as a novel the kind of attention short-story collections seldom command. Consequently, it is the work most frequently attached to Taylor's name in literary histories and surveys, though it is now out of print and virtually unobtainable. Perhaps its importance in the canon of Peter Taylor's work will ultimately be determined by the fact that it reveals in an obvious way the very same merits and defects which his short stories—his more significant achievement—contain on a lesser scale.

CHAPTER 4

The Widows of Thornton

I *"A Simple Country Town"*

THE EIGHT stories and one short play included in *The Widows of Thornton* (1954)[1] were all published originally in magazines between November, 1948, and March, 1954. An apprenticeship of at least a dozen years lies behind even the earliest of these pieces, therefore; and it is not surprising to find Peter Taylor emerging as a master craftsman. *The Widows of Thornton,* however, is more than just the next expected step in a promising writer's career. Though *A Long Fourth* and *A Woman of Means* both revealed an unquestioned talent, neither quite fully indicated the precise form in which this talent would find its most congenial expression. Certain longish stories like "The Scoutmaster" and "A Long Fourth" suggested, for instance, that the novel might be the natural genre for the channeling of Peter Taylor's gifts. But *A Woman of Means,* appealing as it was in many of its parts, did not have essentially novelistic virtues. Stories like "Allegiance" or "Sky Line" held the promise that Taylor might break ground with experimental techniques; stories like "The Fancy Woman" and "A Spinster's Tale" hinted that he might explore unusual or aberrant sociological and psychological situations. In short, Peter Taylor's second story collection might have been any number of things.

What is so amazing about *The Widows of Thornton* is the artistic homogeneity of the pieces in it: it is as if the writer had never for one moment considered any other approaches, as if his mature style and themes had been born fully formed, Venus-like, from the muddy foam of the Tennessee River. Gone are the arty mannerisms which sometimes marred the stories in *A Long Fourth* and the novel *A Woman of Means.* The plot situations in *The Widows of Thornton* avoid not only the slightly melodramatic contrivances and vaguely Gothic settings of "Allegiance" and "A Spinster's Tale" but even the credible but too overtly dramatic confrontations and reversals of works like "A Long Fourth" and *A Woman of Means.* Chronology is still much manipulated as it was, for example, in "The Scoutmaster"; but there is no sense of avant garde distortion or neo-Proustian experimentation. Characterization is fully but economically developed in nearly all the stories, so that characters who at first glance suggest a familiar "type" end as authentic individuals with unique personalities. The first-person point of view, awkward even when handled with Taylor's skill, is avoided entirely. The style steers clear of the tense deliberateness which made stories like "Allegiance" and "Sky Line" sound self-consciously literary and settles instead into the comfortable leisureliness—colloquial and apparently digressive—which had already distinguished "The Scoutmaster" and "A Long Fourth." In short, Taylor's technical prowess has become so controlled in *The Widows of Thornton* that there is the illusion of almost complete artlessness.

The thematic concerns, moreover, are narrowed considerably in *The Widows of Thornton* from the comparatively wide-ranging interests of *A Long Fourth,* leading fortunately to new depths of perception. The original conception of the book was more sociological than the final product, according to Taylor's own account:

> My idea . . . was to write a group of stories dealing with the histories of four or five families from a country town [Thornton, Tennessee] who had migrated, during a period of twenty-five years, to various cities of the South and the Midwest. . . . I wanted to present these families—both Negro and white—living a modern urban life while continuing to be aware of their old identities and relationships. I wanted to give the reader the impression that every character carried in his head a map of that simple country town while going about his life in the complex city . . . to show, in fact, how old patterns, for good or bad, continued to dominate many aspects of these people's lives. In writing the individual stories I discovered new themes in them and found that I sometimes wanted to write directly about the old town itself.[2]

Taylor stuck to his original plan in that he set two of the pieces in St. Louis, two in Nashville, one each in Detroit and Chicago, and one on a train outside Memphis. Though all the stories have characters who apparently derive from Thornton, only two—

"What You Hear From 'Em?" and "Cookie"—have the principal action set in the town of Thornton itself.

The socio-cultural themes which do emerge from the volume, however, are hardly Faulknerian in their impact. *The Widows of Thornton,* in fact, has even less of the epic-style mythologizing so often associated with the "Southern school" of modern fiction than had some of the stories in *A Long Fourth.* It is true that Thornton—"the old, dying town on the bluffs above the Tennessee River"—is a pervasive presence in the lives of all the characters, just as its prototype—Trenton, Tennessee, Taylor's birthplace—has been in Taylor's life. It is also true that the town has a symbolic significance.

As Sylvia Harrison realizes at the climax of "The Dark Walk," life in the strange, vague cities where rural Southerners today so often find themselves exists only as the opposite of something else—the remembered life of a particular place of origin, like Thornton:

> It was there that she had known the name and quality of everything. It was there, more than anywhere else, that everything had a name. Not only the streets and alleys there had had names; there had been names for the intersections of streets: Wifeworking Corner, the Blocks, the Stepdown. Not only the great houses and small houses had names; on the outskirts of the town were two abandoned barns knowns as the Hunchback's Barn and General Forrest's Stable. (301-2)

Thornton provides for these stories what Eudora Welty has defined as "place": "the named, identified, concrete, exact and exacting, and therefore credible, gathering-spot of all that's been felt, is about to be experienced" in the progress of a fiction. "The moment the place in which the novel happens is accepted as true, through it will begin to glow in a kind of recognizable glory the feeling and thought that inhabited the novel in the author's head and animated the whole of his work," Miss Welty has said.[3]

Thornton is then perhaps more a technical device to provide a sense of actuality and an organic thematic unity—like the fictional Morgana, Mississippi, in Miss Welty's story collection *The Golden Apples*—than a mythic reality to provide a transcendence of time and place—like Jefferson in Faulkner's Yoknapatawpha saga. If there is something mythic in the structure of Taylor's story collection, it is more likely the image of the family than the image of the town. For Taylor once again reveals himself obsessed with domestic relationships: the interplay of parents, children, servants, dependent kinfolk. The household of a fictional family like the Tollivers or the Wades is not the statistically average four and one-half persons; the numbers are swollen by extra children, uncles, aunts, assorted other female relatives, maids, chauffeurs, cooks, houseboys. The family may indeed have a compelling sense of its own identity (witness the rallying of the Wades around an estranged relative in "Death of a Kinsman"), an image of its past history and future destiny. Even here, however, the mythic element is muted, compared to that in a Faulkner or a Robert Penn Warren; Thomas Sutpen and Cass Masterson would be totally out of place in Taylor's world.

Probably Taylor's interest in *The Widows of Thornton* has narrowed itself down to the individual person rather than the social unit, even though the individual is never distilled from his socio-cultural and familial context. Except for a few outstanding creations (Harriet Wilson, say, or Uncle Jake), the characters in *A Long Fourth* are not remembered so well as the situations or events; but the characters of *The Widows of Thornton* (Aunt Munsie, Old Ben Bradley, Helen Ruth Lovell, Miss Betty Pettigru, Sylvia Harrison) are individuals we may feel we know even when we've forgotten the details of their stories. Part of the reason for this impression is that we accumulate a greater wealth of detail about these characters in the course of a more leisurely narration, but another equally important part of the reason is that we have been given unusual insights into the depths of their individual personalities.

The insights Taylor does give are not always crystal clear; full understanding of his themes remains a difficult goal. More than before, however, the ambiguities seem less the result of willful obscurity than an unavoidable consequence of unplumbable complexities in the subject matter. Taylor seems much more concerned in this book to say the things he has directly observed in his own special milieu than to repeat the conventional judgments of today's Southern writer about Southern decline and decay.

II *"All That Was Old and Useless and Inherited"*

The story which best represents the special qualities of *The Widows of Thornton* is "The Dark Walk," the last (and the longest) story of the volume. This story most explicitly presents the unifying theme and explains the title of the whole collection, which (it turns out) is not a literal description of the heroines but a startling metaphor.

"The Dark Walk" is the story of Sylvia Harrison, the only actual widow in the book. Sylvia is introduced at an apparently inconsequential but quite revealing point in her life where many of her traits are brought into relief. The time is the mid-1930's when Sylvia is already the mother of four children, the oldest of whom is sixteen. The reader discovers her at an insufferably old-fashioned Colorado resort—the kind of place where entertainment consists of a depressing Saturday night dance where "twelve-year-old girls, still wearing sashes and patent-leather pumps, danced with their grandfathers" and "worse still, old ladies danced together and 'broke' on each other."

The reason that Sylvia Harrison has chosen this resort instead of Colorado Springs (which the "sensible" parents of her children's school friends chose) is a key to Sylvia's character. This resort, it seems, is run by old Miss Katty Moore, who is a native of Sylvia's home state of Tennessee and who had taught gymnastics ("the art of swinging Indian clubs") at Ward-Belmont School in Nashville when Sylvia was a student there. Grotesquely formidable as she now is (shingled snow-white hair, white satin evening dress with low-quarter, white tennis shoes, eyes coyly rolling back into her head until only the whites show), the incredibly muscular old lady is to Sylvia an "association" with the past, something to write to her old schoolmates about, something of Tennessee carried over into the present life. As Sylvia is gradually revealed to the reader, it becomes obvious that the loyalty to old Miss Katty is just one manifestation of a deeply ingrained character trait in Sylvia.

Sylvia has developed her attitude toward Tennessee over the course of many moves throughout the South and Midwest as the career of her husband, Nate, took him to bigger and bigger jobs and to larger and larger cities. Always in these moves, ever since the first one from Cedar Springs to Memphis, Sylvia has carted some four vans of furniture—"almost everything in the way of furniture that her family or Nate's had ever owned." She has developed what is almost a mystique about moving, baffling friends and family by her "untroubled and independent spirit at moving time," organizing the logistics of the move all by herself, priding herself on her efficient technique. Though some things remain ever crated in attic or warehouse, the furniture she transfers from house to house always dominates any new interior so that any individuality is completely obscured and her family can hardly realize its surroundings have been changed. "Home was not Chicago or Detroit, or any of the other places they had lived," Sylvia thus implies. "Home was the old Harrison place at Cedar Springs, or perhaps Sylvia's own family house at Thornton." Furthermore, there is always the understanding that some day they will go back to Tennessee.

Life in the Tennessee small town from whence Sylvia and her husband came is not, however, very appealing in the real-life examples Sylvia sees in the homes of her old acquaintances. She inevitably pities her old schoolmates, finding that the typical husband seems almost not to be there at all, to have "retired from the social scene in Thornton," to be insisting on his right to be like other modern men while demanding at the same time that "his wife, Sylvia's girlhood friend, must continue to live as she always has." Strangely, Sylvia recalls Nate's saying when they were first engaged that "everything changes so fast in our country that a smart person can't hold on to the past—not to any part of it if he wants to be a success." Still, she cherishes the "bittersweet tone" of the "pleasant, prosperous, pastoral surroundings" of Middle Tennessee *circa* 1915, where "she had seen everything that was good in the noble past of her country meeting head on with everything that was exciting and marvelous about the twentieth century."

Sylvia's reassessment of her attitudes is necessitated by the sudden death of her husband in Chicago in 1939 when she is forty-four. Everyone assumes, of course, that Sylvia will now make the long-intended return to Tennessee; and she herself begins dutiful preparations. About this point, though, Sylvia begins to entertain separately two masculine callers who come to represent two sides of her dilemma to her. The first caller is her elderly landlord, Mr. Canada, an undeclared suitor who tries to persuade her to stay in Chicago. The other is Leander, the Negro chauffeur who was one of the servants accompanying Sylvia from Cedar Springs in her first move twenty years earlier and who now is asking her to let him go back to Tennessee with her. Sylvia's children tease her about her "Black Knight" and her "White Knight," but Sylvia sees the two men as representing for her "the two sides of a rather simple question, the question of whether or not it was wise of her to be taking her family back to Tennessee."

At first concerned about her own selfishness, Sylvia eventually realizes that neither side of the question is really her own:

> *She* had no side, no voice in the argument, and had never had one. The two voices she had been listening to for weeks past had both been Nate's voice. They were voices she had heard for years and years. The two men, quarreling in her back hall, seemed to represent the two sides of Nate. He had, through all the years, *wanted* her to *want* to go back to Tennessee. That was what his tolerance had meant. Her own wishes had never entered into it. That was what Nate's tolerance had meant. It had meant his freedom from a part of himself, a part of himself that would have bound him to a place and to a past time otherwise inescapable. He had *wanted* her to insist upon taking all that furniture everywhere they went. . . . She felt now an immense weariness, felt as though she had been carrying all that absurd furniture on her back these twenty years. And for what purpose? Why, so that Nate might be free to live that part of life in which there somehow must be no furniture. His selfishness, for the moment, seemed so monstrous to her that she almost smiled at the judgments she had passed upon herself. (298)

With this new awareness, Sylvia reaches her decision: she sends the vans of furniture and Leander back to Tennessee without her, and she takes a brand new apartment in Chicago to be filled with "new and useful and pleasing" furnishings which she herself will select. She will retain nothing to remind her "of the necessity there had been to dispense with all that was old and useless and inherited."

III *"All, Somehow, Widows"*

"The Dark Walk" would have been interesting enough if this were the extent of its revelations. But embodied in the telling of the story are two significant images which lead to further meanings. The first is the image which provided the title for the story; the second is the image which provides the title for the whole volume. The Dark Walk is the overgrown riverside path in Thornton where courting couples used to stroll, the very spot where Nate had proposed. Besides its association with romantic bliss, the Dark Walk has a more sinister connotation: "an element of mystery and danger . . . in the bright colored spiders which sometimes spun their webs across the path or in the fat water moccasins hurrying innocently across the path into the rank growth of creeper and poison ivy." It is the recalling of these paradoxial associations with the Dark Walk that leads Sylvia to the second key image: the bride-widow paradox.

Ever since her youth, Sylvia has cherished "the image of herself as a young girl in white dimity repeating and sharing the experience of all the other girls to whom life had seemed to begin anew" in the Dark Walk. At the point in her life where she realizes the role she has been forced to play by her husband's silent demands, Sylvia finds the image changed:

> She and the other young girls no longer seemed to be beginning life anew in the Dark Walk. They were all dressed in black, and it seemed that the experience they had shared there was really the beginning of widowhood. From the moment they pledged their love they were all, somehow, widows; and she herself had become a widow not the day Nate was found dead in his office but the day he asked her to marry him, in the Dark Walk. It seemed to her that in some way or other all the men of that generation in that town had been killed in the old war of her grandfather's day. Or they had been set free by it. Or their lives had been changed in a way that the women's lives were not changed. The men of Nate's time had crossed over a border, had pushed into a new country, or fled into a new country. And their brides lived as widows clinging to things the men would never come back to and from which they could not free themselves. Nate had gone literally to a new country, but Sylvia knew in her heart that it would have been the same if they had never left Cedar Springs. (303-4)

Pledging love, then, for a woman in Sylvia's socio-cultural context, means a clinging to the "old and useless and inherited"—the four vans of furniture Sylvia moved from city to city. The men escape to freedom (even the husbands of Sylvia's schoolmates back in Thornton, we remember, have retired from the scene, seeming almost not to be there at all), but Sylvia and the other wives must live as they always have. The "Widows of Thornton" are the futile bearers of vain tradition in a changing modern world.

The majority of the stories in *The Widows of Thornton* can be seen as more or less related extensions of this central theme, Two other stories directly concern wives who are in Sylvia's sense "somehow widows," and three others deal with various women who, in pledging their love, were led to cling to something from which they might otherwise have been free.

One of the simplest stories in the volume, "Cookie" (originally entitled "Middle Age"), takes on a significance in the context of the whole volume that it probably would not have alone. It presents a wife who is a very paragon of patience and servility trying to preserve the slender ties that still bind her philandering doctor-husband to her. "Two nights a week, he *had* to be home for supper, and some weeks, when his conscience was especially uneasy, he turned up three or four times," the story begins; and we meet the husband and wife at a typical evening meal. The dull chronic tensions between the two are subtly revealed underneath ritualistic conversational banalities:

> He served himself from the dish of beans and selected a piece of the side meat. He bent his head over and got one whiff of the steaming dish. "You're too good to me," he said evenly. He pushed the dish across the table to within her reach.
>
> "Nothing's too good for one's husband."
>
> "You're much too good to me," he said, now lowering his eyes to his plate. (152)

The dramatic catalyst in the story is the title character, the Negro cook, who is completely dedicated to her mistress. Goaded by the petty teasing of her mistress' husband, Cookie cunningly lets slip, in feigned innocence, an illusion to the husband's infidelities, bringing into the open what had before been hidden. Both husband and wife, however, choose to take the indiscretion as an example of "old-nigger uppitiness" and to ignore its implications for their own situation. As the wife goes out to remonstrate with Cookie, the doctor-husband flees the house once more, reflecting on their "ugly, old voices," their "senseless voices"—"the righteousness and disillusion of Cookie's, the pride and discipline of his wife's." Like Nate in "The Dark Walk," he leaves his wife behind, a virtual prisoner in her conventional home; and he turns himself toward the symbol of his own escape: "In the driveway, his car, bright and new and luxurious, was waiting for him."

Just as the wives in "The Dark Walk" and in "Cookie" are figurative widows without knowing it, so too is the heroine of "A Wife of Nashville." The title appropriately focuses our attention on what is of most evident significance about her: first, her social role as wife; second, her cultural context of Southern city life. Her name, Helen Ruth, suggests that she contains at least potentially the contrasting attributes of both of the great prototypes of wifehood: the faithless pagan Helen and the faithful biblical Ruth. Helen Ruth is, in fact, a study in that debilitating kind of vague female dissatisfaction that Betty Friedan was to popularize, fifteen years after this story was written, in *The Feminine Mystique*.

Developed as a seemingly anecdotal chronicle of a housewife's dealings with various household servants over a period of more than twenty years, "A Wife of Nashville" only gradually reveals its underlying pattern. As Helen Ruth frets in turn over lazy Jane Blakemoor, shifty and negligent Carrie, religious but amorous Sarah, and devoted but deceptive Jess McGeehee, she is really fretting over her own lot as wife. "It seemed to her then that she had so little in life that she was entitled to the satisfaction of keeping an orderly house and to the luxury of efficient help," we are told. "There was too much else she had not had—an 'else' nameless to her, yet sorely missed—for her to be denied these small satisfactions." The Negro servants always eventually leave her house; their length of service ranges from nearly three years to a full eight years. Even Jess McGeehee, who "idealized the family" and kept a scrapbook on the accomplishments of Helen Ruth's three boys, finally sets up an elaborate subterfuge and departs for California. But, except for a brief and only vaguely defined separation once in the early years of her marriage, Helen Ruth has remained tied to her household, despite her wistful yearning for a nameless "so much else."

The irony is that the whole world, including presumably Helen Ruth's own husband and children, believes her marriage ideal. "It's too bad more marriages can't be like theirs, each living their own life," a friend observes. "Everyone admires it as a real achievement." But it is the fact that in actuality only John R., Helen Ruth's husband, leads an independent life that irks Helen Ruth. It is John R., away most of the week on business, who runs away at other times on hunting and fishing trips, who takes her only to parties with his hunting friends, and who, when at home, piles up on the bed after supper and sleeps. (Only for a brief period during the Depression when John R. "had to give up all his 'activities' and devote his entire time to selling insurance," did Helen Ruth find herself "spending all her evenings playing Russian bank with a man who had no interest in anything but his home, his wife, and his three boys." But during this period, John R. develops psychosomatic back pains.)

Helen Ruth at first believed that she was "perfectly happy with her present life" but that John R. must be "unhappy" since he seemed no longer to enjoy her company. Hence there was more than once some talk of separation and divorce during the first two years of their marriage and even one actual brief separation when Helen Ruth returned to Thornton with her two babies and Carrie. "Their reconciliation, whatever it meant to John R., meant to her the acceptance of certain mysteries—the mystery of his love of hunting, of his choice of friends, of his desire to maintain a family and home of which he saw so little, of his attachment to her, and of her own devotion to him."

If Helen Ruth had had the insight granted to Sylvia Harrison in "The Dark Walk," she might have penetrated the sociological center of these "mysteries." As it is, she submits to the specious reasoning of her women friends: "Because a woman's husband hunts is no reason for her to hunt, any more than because a man's wife sews is any reason for him to sew." Only when the final Negro servant, Jess McGeehee, the one they had thought would one day be called "Mammy" by future grandchildren, leaves them does Helen Rose plumb something of her life's "mysteries"; but her insight is psychological rather than sociological.

As the only member of the family who discovers Jess's reasons for leaving, Helen Ruth tries to explain the unexpected departure to her husband and sons. Why should Jess, who had "no life of her own," pack up and leave forever her beloved white family? The answer is, of course, that it is too unnatural for anyone, even a Jess McGeehee or a Helen Ruth Lovell, to have *no* life of her own. But the answer is also to be found in the essential "lonesomeness" that people feel. Helen Ruth feels she would gladly draw illustrations from her own life if she could only make her family understand:

> If it would make them see what she had been so long in learning to see, she would even talk at last about the "so much else" that

> had been missing from her life and that she had not been able to name, and about the foolish mysteries she had so nobly accepted upon her reconciliation with John R. To her, these things were all one now; they were her loneliness, the loneliness from which everybody, knowingly or unknowingly, suffered. But she knew that her husband and her sons did not recognize her loneliness or Jess McGeehee's or their own. (98)

Despairing of communicating her insight to her family, Helen Ruth finally turns away from the "identical expressions, not of wonder but of incredulity" on the masculine faces; and she pushes her teacart into the dining room, the symbolic center of her and Jess McGeehee's lives. The dining room is "spotlessly clean, the way Jess McGeehee had left it," but it is also—as the visible representation of the frigid widowish underworld to which a wife of Nashville is doomed—a kind of dark walk, "dark and cool as an underground cavern."

It is part of Peter Taylor's artistry that a story such as this is not reducible to just another post-Ibsenite plea to release latter-day Noras from their doll houses. There are no polemics in "A Wife of Nashville" or in the other stories of *The Widows of Thornton;* there are almost no judgments or commentaries on the situations so skillfully elucidated. Sylvia Harrison in "The Dark Walk" is the only heroine who makes a rebellious decision, and even this decision comes when the circumstances have already substantially changed. The wives in "Cookie" and "A Wife of Nashville" merely endure their situations, which, perhaps, they have come to understand a little better. If Southern family customs make all wives widows in their husband's houses, Peter Taylor is not quixotic enough to offer a panacea for the problem.

IV *"They Ought To Come Home"*

Perhaps Taylor's reticence is in deference to the complexity and extensiveness of the problem. As several other pieces in *The Widows of Thornton* show, the metaphoric widowhood may fall on others besides actual wives. Old family servants, dependent maiden aunts, rich benefactresses, and devoted daughters and nieces can also—by "pledging their love" to a family—enter the dark walk to spiritual widowhood, clinging to things the rest of the world values no more.

One of the most interesting of these stories—a prize-winner which reveals the depth with which Taylor knows the society he chooses to write about—is "What You Hear From 'Em?"—the story of Aunt Munsie, the aged Negro servant of one of the "quality" families in Thornton, that of Dr. Tolliver. "Without being able to book-read or even to make numbers, she had finished raising the whole pack of towheaded Tollivers just as the Mizziz would have wanted it done," we are told. "The Doctor told her she *had to*—he didn't ever think about getting another wife, or taking in some cousin, not after his 'Molly darling'—and Aunt Munsie *did*." In the "halcyon days after the old Mizziz had died," Aunt Munsie's word had actually "become law in the Tolliver household."

The story deals, however, with the period of the 1920's after Aunt Munsie's white charges have grown up, moved away, and begun families of their own. It is the moving away which has most grieved Munsie and which prompts the reiterated question she poses to the few remaining white people who understand it: "What you hear from 'em?" By this question, she wants to know only when her two favorites of the Tolliver children, Mr. Thad and Mr. Will, are going to "pack up their families and come back to Thornton for good." The letters, the Christmas presents, and the occasional ritual visits she gets from Mr. Thad and Mr. Will and their families mean nothing to her; she is looking for their permanent return and nothing less satisfies her.

Munsie realizes that the Tolliver boys—like many other Thornton scions "who had gone off somewhere making money"—are "prospering" in their fine businesses in Memphis and Nashville; but she feels that, "if they were going to be rich, they ought to come home, where their granddaddy had owned land and where their money counted for something." Otherwise, they are only like the mill manager from Chicago, who has "a yard full of big cars and a stucco house as big as you like" but whom nobody in Thornton would take for "rich." Though the old Tolliver house, left vacant by the heirs, has long ago burned down, Munsie insists there is still a sharp division between real "quality" families like the Tollivers and "has-been quality," "mill hands," and "strangers from up North who [run] the Piggly Wiggly, the five-and-ten-cent store, and the roller-skating rink."

It is a "conspiracy" which takes place in the town—a conspiracy directed toward Aunt Munsie's own good—which finally forces the old Negro to face the truth. The conspiracy, launched by some of the quality ladies of the town and abetted by Mr. Will or Mr. Thad's intercession with the mayor, is a plot to get a law passed banning pigs in the city limits, so that Aunt Munsie will have no reason to push her traffic-disrupting slop wagon through the streets. Whether or not her own safety was the motivation for the action, Munsie finds the Tolliver part in the conspiracy a revelation. "I tell you what the commotion's about," she says the day she drives away her pigs. "They *ain't* comin' back. They ain't never comin' back. They ain't never had no notion of comin' back." She rejects at the same time any idea that she might go to them because, as she puts it to her collie dog, "I ain't nothin' to 'em in Memphis, and they ain't nothin' to me in Nashville." "*You* can go!" she irately informs the dog. "A collie dog's a collie dog anywhar. But Aunt Munsie, she's just their Aunt Munsie here in Thornton. I got mind enough to see *that*."

Thus, old and ignorant as she is, Aunt Munsie reaches a profound truth about the relative value of social roles. Up to this point she has lived the role her station in the Tolliver family permitted; she had a hard pride and dignity which at least the quality folks in the town could understand. But in the twenty years she lives on after the end of her daily rounds with the slop wagon, in the twenty years remaining before she dies at the reputed age of one hundred, she lives a changed role. People say she has "softened," for she laughs and hollers with the white folks on the Square "the way they liked her to," takes to tying a bandanna about her head, begins talking "old-nigger foolishness," reminisces about the Civil War and about old days in the Tolliver family, maintains a new formality toward Mr. Thad and Mr. Will and their families, and never again asks any more about when they are "sure enough coming back." Recognizing that the context for her role has disappeared, she has, in short, adapted at the age of eighty-two to the circumstances of a changing world.

"What You Hear From 'Em?" is several kinds of story at once. It is one of the few works written by a white man which does any kind of justice to the psychology of the Southern Negro; it ranks in this respect with such acknowledged masterpieces as Faulkner's "That Evenin' Sun," Eudora Welty's "Livvie," and Reynolds Price's "The Warrior Princess Ozimba." Not just Munsie, but her daughter Crecie (a dramatic contrast to Munsie in personality and attitudes) and the whole complex of white-Negro relationships in the small-town South come to life in this appealing story. Most importantly, the Scylla and Charybdis that beset the usual story in this genre—the opposite dangers of sentimental idealization and nervous condescension—are both avoided.

The story is also a paean to human dignity, a comment on social stratifications, and a lament for the passing of the small town. And, finally, it is a variation on the "widowhood" theme of the previous stories. This time we realize that the movement of the sons of the South into a "new country" leaves more than their wives clinging to the "old and useless and inherited," and that not the least of those things which are "old and useless and inherited" are social roles adapted to a context that will never be revived.

V "*How This Family Business Works*"

Successful accommodations to changed contexts can sometimes be made—at least for a while, as the one short play in *The Widows of Thornton* demonstrates. *The Death of a Kinsman* is the dramatization of a crucial moment in the life of an expatriate Tennessee family in Detroit, a moment when carefully preserved "roles" are brought up for reexamination. The large Wade household—consisting of Robert, his wife Margie, his Aunt Lida, his five children, and three Negro servants—has managed to preserve in alien surroundings a Southern way of life based on models of an earlier day. The most delicate roles, those which have to be enacted with the greatest tact and consciousness of the unwritten rules, are of course the ones of the wife and the dependent female relative: the traditionally problematic two women under one roof.

Fortunately, Margie and Aunt Lida play their roles without a cross word to mar the family serenity. "It's because we have arranged our lives as we have," Mrs. Wade explains to her husband. "It's Because Aunt Lida and I have played our roles so perfectly, as we've always seen them played in Tennessee: She, the maiden aunt, responsible and capable! I, the beautiful young wife, the bearer of children, the reigning queen!" Conceivably, the arrangement might have lasted indefinitely; but an external force challenges it.

This force is the opinion of the modern, urban, non-Southern culture, represented in the person of Miss Bluemeyer, the Yankee housekeeper. When I selected Miss Bluemeyer for Margie's housekeeper," Aunt Lida says, "I was careful to choose someone who wouldn't fit in. If she were congenial with us, her presence here would be an intrusion. That's why my presence is an intrusion, don't you see?" Being totally outside the Southern tradition, Miss Bluemeyer has difficulty recognizing the clearly defined "spheres of authority" in the house and seems to the Wades "critical and questioning of a happy family life."

The death of an estranged and misanthropic relative, a Cousin Harry Wilson, is the event which brings Miss Bluemeyer and Aunt Lida into open conflict. With typical Southern concern for the obligations of "kinship," the Wades begin the obsequies for Cousin Harry, much to the mystification of Miss Bluemeyer. The housekeeper at first thinks the Wades are "such wonderful people to feel so responsible for a person they hardly know," but she later judges that they are only fawning over a relative in an impersonal and meaningless Southern ritual. Believing that she is the only one who has any concern for the dead man as a person, Miss Bluemeyer sends flowers anonymously to the funeral service, a gesture which brings only a snide rebuff from Aunt Lida.

"What is it about Miss Bluemeyer's queerness that disturbs Aunt Lida so?" Robert Wade innocently asks, and Margie replies: "It is only that someone has entered the field who won't play the game according to Aunt Lida's rules." Aunt Lida puts it another way; it is people like the embittered Cousin Harry and Miss Bluemeyer, she says, who make the role-playing "hard," who "point an accusing finger." Inevitably, the confrontation of the two women must occur, and when it does Miss Bluemeyer dramatically gives her notice:

> MISS BLUEMEYER: . . . I understand a good deal of how this family business works. It makes a woman safe and sure being related this way and that way to everybody around her. And it keeps you from having to bother about anybody else, since they are not "kinfolks." I understand how it works, for I was one of nine, and I saw the women in my family making the most of it too. And I might have done the same, but I was a queer sort who couldn't make herself do it.

Aunt Lida: Is that all, Miss Bluemeyer?

Miss Bluemeyer: Not quite all. For a solid year I have watched you here giving directions and making this house your own. And I have seen it right along that you are really the same as I in lots of your feelings, Miss Wade, that you are really lost and alone in the world, but you would not have it so, you just wouldn't. All along I have seen you are really a brainy woman and yet to see you here saying the things you say and play-acting all the time! And then when the old man Wilson was dying, you, like the rest of 'em, talked of nothing but that he was kin, kin, kin. You have mocked and joked all this day and gave him a funeral only because he was a kinsman. (147-48)

The point of the play, then, is that Aunt Lida and Miss Bluemeyer are indeed "really the same" in many ways—only the accommodation each has made to circumstances has been different. Aunt Lida has chosen the way of the Southern gentlewoman, assuming the role of dependent relative with its small prerogatives and large heartaches. But this role is possible only by clinging to the remnants of a lost past—the familiar plight of Taylor's other "widows." Miss Bluemeyer, on the other hand, has chosen the way Southern men of the past few generations (but not Southern women) have been choosing: the way of independent enterprise in a mobile society. To the Southern-bred woman, Miss Bluemeyer's way seems a reveling in "bitterness" and a despising of all those who try to make life "a less lonesome, a less dreary business," while to the Northern-bred woman, Aunt Lida's way seems an abject surrender of all "pride and independence."

VI *"Life's Most Important Lessons"*

One story, "Two Ladies in Retirement," presents both alternatives successively in the same woman. The woman is Miss Betty Pettigru, a Nashville society leader for twenty-five years who suddenly retires with a female cousin and close companion to the home of some relatives in St. Louis. One of the most memorable characters Taylor has created (she appears again in the play *Tennessee Day in St. Louis*), Miss Betty is a combination of Aunt Lida's craving for familial affection and Miss Bluemeyer's yen for independence. Unfortunately, she has the Southern woman's usual difficulty in realizing both desires.

In Nashville, Miss Betty had made the most of her none-too-promising opportunities. As "the unbeautiful, untalented heiress of a country family's fortune" removed from the "decaying and disappearing" country town (Thornton) which gave that fortune its only meaning, she had little chance of fulfilling her father's injunction to make her "place" in "the heart of some gentle, honest man." Instead, she did what a man might have done:

> The men of her generation, and of later generations, had gone to Nashville, Memphis, Louisville, and even to St. Louis, and had used their heads, their connections, and their genteel manners to make their way to the top in the new order of things. And wasn't that all *she* had done, and in the only way permissible for a Miss Pettigru from Thornton? Once the goal was defined, was it necessary that she should be any less ruthless than her male counterparts? In her generation, the ends justified the means. For men, at least, they did. Now, at last, Miss Betty saw how much like a man's life her own had been. (186-87)

What Miss Betty had done was to build her life on a hard-headed personal goal—social climbing—through a ruthless process of what her companion Flo Dear thought of as "sin and expiation, sin and expiation, but with never a resolution to sin no more" and what she herself thought of as "life, plain and simple, where you did what good things you could and what bad things you must."

Finally, facing at last the fact of the "worthlessness" of the goal which circumstances and personal limitations had set for her, Miss Betty abandoned Nashville society to take up permanent residence with the James Tolliver family in St. Louis where she could hope to indulge time, money, and love on three young nephews. Here, however, as the story opens, Miss Betty finds she has strong competition for the favor of the three Tolliver boys. Her rival, ironically enough, is Vennie, the Tollivers' aging cook, who lures the children with special treats cooked on her "magic stove" in her basement apartment and captivates them with exciting stories about old times in Thornton.

There is little doubt that Miss Betty will eventually triumph over old Vennie; the question is "To what means will she stoop to do it?" The temptation to win a quick victory by slightly less than honorable methods is not long in coming, and it comes from a particularly charming tempter, one of the very prizes over whom the contest is being waged. Vance, the oldest boy, has been offended, it seems, by some of Vennie's joshing in front of his school friends. Sensing Auntie Bet's own attitude toward Vennie, he gives her the opportunity to eavesdrop through a hot-air register on "carryings-on" in Vennie's apartment and insinuates that incriminating evidence sufficient to dispose of Vennie can be obtained.

But Miss Betty Pettigru, who has not hesitated in the past to use the power of the blackball or the weapon of the impeachment clause to bully out a victory in Nashville club circles, is truly shocked that Vance had seen she was capable of low tactics and had thought she might "enter into a conspiracy with little children in the house of her kinspeople." She is brought to the realization that women are bound by a more stringent moral order than men: "Wrong though it seemed, the things a man did to win happiness in the world—or in the only world Miss Betty knew—were of no consequence to the children he came home to at night, but every act, word and thought of a woman was judged by and reflected in the children, in the husband, in all who loved her" (187). And Miss Betty, for her "new start in life," has chosen the kind of domesticity where a woman's moral decisions matter most. When the final exposure of Vennie comes, Miss Betty has had no direct hand in it.

Miss Betty is not the only one to derive insights from the Vennie episode. Her cousin and companion, the gentle and timid Flo Dear, also reaches an important moral realization: "It seemed to her that perhaps to do anything at all in the world was to do wrong to *someone*." Her own way of life has been essentially passive and therefore not very harmful to others, but she now judges Miss Betty more kindly; for Miss Betty, by the very activeness of her love, seemed bound to hurt someone. Further, though Flo Dear has long been an authority on Tennessee genealogy, she only at this point seems to have sensed the full significance of family love in qualifying moral relationships. At the end of the story, at any rate, we have the image of Flo Dear elucidating to the three boys "just exactly what her family connection was with them, and in even greater detail . . . the blood ties that existed between them and their Auntie Bet." And the boys, we are told, listened attentively, "as though they were learning life's most important lessons."

VII *"A Past Era, A Better Era"*

What is almost a compendium of such "important lessons" is found in another story of family ties, "Their Losses," the first entry in the volume. A Pullman car on a Southern Railroad train en route westward from Grand Junction, Tennessee, to Memphis is the setting which brings together three Tennessee women who vigorously debate the moral reasons for mourning or not mourning over family deaths. Each of the three has just experienced or is about to experience the death of a close relative. Miss Patty Bean of Thornton is bringing home an aged and mentally ill aunt to spend her last days "where she is greatly loved." Miss Ellen Louise Watkins of Brownsville is escorting her mother's body from Sweetwater, where she died, to Brownsville, where she will be buried. And Mrs. Cornelia Weatherby Werner of Memphis is just returning from Grand Junction where she put her old mother "to her last rest."

The three women's reactions to "their losses" are quite varied. Miss Ellen's attitude is the most conventional; she believes in mourning as the sentimental response which love naturally motivates. Cornelia, on the other hand, refuses to mourn the death of her own mother, who, she says, was "opinionated and narrow and mentally cruel to her children and her husband" and "tied to things that were over and done with before she was born." Her position is like Miss Ellen's, however, in that she makes the propriety of the mourning depend on the worthiness of the person lost. It is Miss Patty who articulates a purely rationalistic defense of the custom of mourning.

"Mourning is an obligation," Miss Patty tells the others. "We only mourn those with whom we have some real connection, people who have represented something important and fundamental in our lives." She makes it clear that she is not speaking of wearing black—the "symbol" of mourning—but of the mourning itself. "I shall mourn the loss of my aunt when she goes, because she is my aunt, because she is the last of my aunts, and particularly because she is an aunt who has maintained a worthwhile position in the world," she says, insisting that how she regarded the members of her family as individuals is "neither here nor there." "My family happened to be very much *of* the world," Miss Patty adds. "Not of *this* world but of *a* world that we have seen disappear. In mourning my family, I mourn that world's disappearance."

That world is, of course, the world of the vanishing towns the train has been passing through. The towns, the three women have agreed, were "good towns," "fine towns," "lovely towns," with "the atmosphere of a prosperous and civilized existence." These towns contrast sharply with a modern metropolis like Memphis, which Miss Patty avers she never liked; Miss Ellen says never liked her; and Cornelia, who lives there, admits is a "wretched place," where "they can't forgive you for being from the country." The significance of the small towns is that they—or at least the women in them, Taylor's metaphoric widows—have "wanted to retain the standards of a past era, a better era."

VIII *"Not as People But as Symbols"*

The remaining two stories in *The Widows of Thornton* also take up cultural contrasts, but represent them in characters of different generations. "Porte-Cochere" presents the antagonistic relationship between an elderly father and one of his sons, and "Bad Dreams" details an equally antagonistic relationship between a young Negro servant couple and an aged Negro tramp who intrudes on their domestic privacy. In the first story, we see the circumstances largely through the older person's point of view; in the second, primarily through the young people's.

Old Ben Brantley in "Porte-Cochere" is a crochety egocentric of seventy-six years who badgers petulantly the five children who come back to Nashville to visit him on his birthday. From his study (opening on the landing halfway between the first and second floors of his house), above the porte-cochere, Old Ben can spy on his children whether they are in the yard, on the side-porch, or in the house; and he can snare their attention to himself any time they use the stairs. In an orgy of self-pity, Old Ben thinks: "What would old age be without children? Desolation, desolation. But what would old age be with children who chose to ignore the small demands that he would make upon them, that he had ever made upon them? A nameless torment!" His older son Clifford, whom he particularly harasses, can only wonder at his father's motives and desires: "It's your children that have got old, and you've stayed young—and not in any good sense, Papa, only in a bad one! You play sly games with us still or you quarrel with us. What the hell do you want of us, Papa? I've thought about it a lot. Why haven't you ever asked for what it is you want? Or are *we* all blind and it's really obvious?"

Old Ben's memories of his own childhood supply us with some of the answer. Suffering under the harsh discipline of a cruel father, Ben in his youth had vowed to "go away to another country . . . where there would be no children and no fathers." Wanting his own house "to be as different from his father's house as a house could be," he has given his own children a freedom he had never known but has "tortured and plagued them in all the ways that his resentment of their very good fortune had taught him to do." In a gesture of senile despair and frustration, he draws out the very stick (with his father's bearded face carved on it) with which his father used to beat him and flays the chairs of his room while "calling the names of his children under his breath."

In "Bad Dreams" Taylor gives us the equally frustrated desires of youth to protect itself from the demands of old age. Emmaline and Bert, maid and houseboy for the James Tolliver family in St. Louis, are highly resentful when Mr. Tolliver brings a disreputable old Thornton Negro to share the servants' quarters with them and their four-month-old nameless baby. Realizing all too well that the old man, once deposited upon them, will be their complete responsibility, Emmaline and Bert make vague plans to "get shed of" the old man. Only when the unsavory old-timer helps them out of a middle-of-the-night crisis with a shrieking and gasping baby—he convinces them the child was not sick but only had "bad dreams"—is an uncertain reconciliation of the two generations effected.

The old man has represented many things to Bert and Emmaline. He is the image of "all the poverty and nigger life" they had escaped when they left Thornton for St. Louis. He is an overt threat to their humble aspirations—to keep their baby with them and to convert the extra servant's room into a nursery. He is a reminder of the humiliations a Negro must suffer at the hands of whites. When the old man explains the baby's nightmare—"I reckon he thought the boogyman after him"—he is also explaining Bert and Emmaline's reaction to himself and the dreams from which they had been awakened.

Yet Taylor specifically warns that it may be necessary for us to treat such "pathetic old tramps," who have somehow "moved beyond the reach of the human imagination" in their unlikeness to us, "not as people but as symbols of something we like or dislike." Their "loneliness" is both the evidence of their estrangement from humanity and the proof of their kinship with it. This passage at the end of the story—a passage that almost abandons the pretense of a character's point of view and speaks with auctorial directness—ends with a reflection that the old man too may have his "bad dreams" like Bert and Emmaline and the nameless baby. The only comfort is that there certainly will not be so many ahead for him as for the others.

Together the two stories, "Porte-Cochere" and "Bad Dreams," suggest once more the mystery of human personality and the terrible barriers to love and understanding even among those with natural affinities. And in the total context of *The Widows of Thornton,* they remind us again of the certain necessity but dubious possibility of trying to preserve those ties—of blood, of love, of history, and of institutions—which alone keep people somehow together even in their loneliness.

CHAPTER 5

From Fiction to Drama

I "The Curtain Rises"

THE EARLY STORIES of Peter Taylor, with their undramatic conflicts, their drawn out characterizations, their dependence upon nuances of descriptive language for the maintenance of authenticity of setting and delicacy of tone, certainly did not hold out any special promise of playwriting talent. Nevertheless, Taylor was moving steadily toward the new genre. Kenneth Clay Cathey, for one, detected a developing dramatic sense in "Allegiance" (1947) and the stories following it.[1] And between the end of the war and the time *A Long Fourth* was published in 1948, Taylor had reportedly already written two plays.[2] Since then Taylor has maintained a steady interest in playwriting, but he has released for publication only one one-act play and two full-length plays.

In the winter of 1949, the first of Taylor's dramatic efforts to be published, *The Death of a Kinsman*, appeared in *Sewanee Review*.[3] As we have already seen, this play, in its single act, develops an interesting variation on the "widowhood" theme which unifies the diverse pieces in *The Widows of Thornton*. In addition, it gives provocative insights into the plight of the transplanted Southerner, into the necessity of role-playing in the achievement of family harmony, and into the multiple and complex relationships which exist between sexes, generations, classes, races, and regions.

As perceptive as the play is thematically, it is nevertheless problematical technically. One-act plays with a cast of twelve are not in great demand—especially when three of the roles are for Negroes and five are for children ranging in age from four to twelve. More limiting still is the set called for: it must simulate the upstairs hall-sitting room of "one of those mansions put up in Midwestern cities during the early part of the present century."

A large stair well is the focus of interest in the center and back of the stage; and around it are oak balustrades, pilasters, and elaborate door facings for the numerous rooms opening off the hall. Details of the furnishings are specified, and it is impossible to imagine an actual set revealing the subtle distinctions called for in the author's stage directions: "The floor is not carpeted, but it is partly covered by two large rugs. The one on the left is a handsome, though rather worn and faded, Oriental rug. On the right is an obviously new imitation of the same thing, with extremely bright colors and a general effect of silkiness." The sociological content of the play certainly demands that the setting be as authentic and realistic as possible.

The chief question about *The Death of a Kinsman,* however, is whether its artistic point can be realized dramaturgically. "The play is obviously experimental," Kenneth Clay Cathey has observed, arguing that "it is incapable of holding an audience's attention throughout an actual stage performance since the entire first half accomplishes nothing but exposition."[4] If Cathey finds the beginning of the play theatrically deficient, Morgan Blum finds an even greater deficiency in "the essentially undramatic quality of its ending." Blum admits that the ending is "based on the kind of self-discovery that is inevitably blurred for many members of a theatre audience because it is difficult to find a clearcut way of presenting, on the stage, anything so essentially inward." But Blum insists that the device Taylor employs to point to this self-discovery by Aunt Lida (a subtle positioning of the characters as the curtain falls) is "unsatisfactory," since it "does not define the play's change, the degree to which the discovery is accepted, with any real precision"—the way, for instance, looking into the character's consciousness might have done it in a short story.[5]

Brainard Cheney, considering the possibility that Taylor's plays may be "fiction . . . in the trappings of plays," concludes that *The Death of a Kinsman* does "*fictional* violence to an axiom of the theater—the maxim that a play must make its points obviously, that it cannot resort to the techniques of indirection practiced in fiction because the spectator has only the passing instant in which to grasp the meaning of the action."[6] Since Cathey, Blum, and Cheney all consider *The Death of a Kinsman* an artistic success of sorts, despite its dramaturgical inadequacies, the conclusion seems to be that Taylor's first play is a rewarding closet drama—not a living theater piece.

II "*A Microcosm of Life Back Home*"

Tennessee Day in St. Louis (1957) repeats a number of the inadequacies of *The Death of a Kinsman*, but it is, by and large, a more satisfactory adjustment to the conventions of the stage.[7] It manages to transfer to the new genre many of the appealing features of Taylor's distinguished short fiction. In the larger expanse of its four acts, it is able to bring life to the Tolliver family to a degree that *The Death of a Kinsman* could not quite manage for the Wades. The intertwinings of familial relationships are certainly as complex here as in any of the longish short stories of the previous books.

The Tolliver family depicted in the play is the same Tolliver family featured in "Two Ladies in Retirement" and alluded to in "Bad Dreams" and other stories of *The Widows of Thornton*. Certain modifications in the Tolliver ménage are, however, apparent. The three sons found in "Two Ladies in Retirement" are here reduced to two, Jim and Lanny (called Jimmy and Landon in the earlier work). Though Vance has disappeared, some of his character traits seem to have been taken over by Lanny (who, incidentally, has also taken over the birthday assigned to Jimmy in "Two Ladies in Retirement"). Only one servant, Bert (who was featured in "Bad Dreams"), appears on stage; but the presence of Emmaline and other Negro help in the off-stage background is implied and not difficult to imagine. Miss Betty Pettigru (called Auntie Bet here) and Flo Dear, her gentle companion, reveal the same basic traits of character they had in "Two Ladies in Retirement." The father of the family, James Tolliver, is likewise consistent with his earlier image. The only character to undergo some transformation is the mother, whose name is changed from Amy to Helen and who seems here more ebullient than before.

Several additional kinfolk have been introduced into the Tolliver household for the play. The most important is Helen's brother William, whose anti-familial ideas provide a direct contrast with his environment. On the periphery of the family is William's mistress, Lucy McDougal, who has been given entrée into the intimate family circle under the fiction that she is William's secretary and fiancée. And visiting the Tollivers over Tennessee Day are a distant cousin of Helen's, Senator Cameron Caswell, and his granddaughter, Nancy. Each of these characters is defined not only by his role in the family but by his attitude toward his role.

The actual happenings of the play are not outwardly momentous, though Lanny's attempted suicide at the end of Act II is at least potentially tragic. Various characters merely pass by each other in the different ritual encounters of family living, protected from too direct confrontations by the conventions which assign complementary roles to all. Only in the brief moments between ritual activities, when the protective conventions are not fully operative, do repressed tensions and antagonisms break forth in mild personal clashes. Yet the occasions are sufficient in the course of the play's single day to bring out conflicts between Lanny and William, William and Lucy, Lucy and Auntie Bet, Auntie Bet and Senator Caswell, and Senator Caswell and Lanny.

What gives significance to the slight happenings of the plot is the socio-cultural context in which they occur. Though the play has its universal values, its action is firmly grounded in a clearly defined interval of historic time and in a clearly specified geographic milieu. The title focuses attention on both time and place: the occasion is Tennessee Day, January 8, 1939; and the locale is St. Louis, Missouri, one of the Midwestern metropolises in which so many of Taylor's old-time Southerners find themselves transplanted but not yet fully acclimated.

Tennessee Day annually celebrates an epic victory by an almost mythic Southerner—the famous Battle of New Orleans in which Andrew Jackson with only six thousand men defeated twelve thousand British troops in 1815. Like many other events of Southern history, the Battle of New Orleans is both incredible and ironic, incredible because Jackson lost only seven men to the British loss of two thousand, ironic because the belated triumph took place two weeks after a peace treaty had been signed. In Peter Taylor's own life, Tennessee Day has added significance; for January 8 is both the date on which his parents were married (in 1908) and the date on which he was born (in 1917). In the play, too, Taylor makes Tennessee Day a triple feast as James and Helen's anniversary and Lanny's birthday. It is no doubt symbolic that the celebration of these two familial and personal occasions of the Tollivers is temporarily quashed in deference to

Senator Caswell, the high priest of the civic holy day.

Senator Caswell is, in fact, the hierophant who elucidates the mysteries of the ritual occasion. The play opens with the Senator rehearsing his Tennessee Day banquet speech and intoning Delphic phrases full of portent and prophecy: "The most frightful of all spectacles, the strength of civilization without its mercy . . . (*Reappearing*) It was artfully contrived by Augustus, that, in the enjoyment of plenty, the Romans should lose the memory of freedom," and "Every generation has its crisis, my friends! But preparation for defense does not always mean war!" As a former poet, lecturer, actor, and literary man, the Senator is a professional interpreter of social history who does not hesitate to expound the meaning he sees in present circumstances. "In the midst of the delights which the modern city offers, you have the delights of the old-fashioned country family," Senator Caswell tells James. "You have your Negro servants and your children and your dependent kinfolks all about you in one house." For him, the Tolliver household is "a sort of microcosm of life back home," where "all the familiar patterns, all the cherished paraphernalia" can be enjoyed without the "responsibility" that went with them in the old environment.

Most of the characters fail to take the Senator and his pronouncements with much seriousness; their attitudes range from William's contemptuous mockery to James's good-humored tolerance. Only Lanny accepts the Senator as seer and prophet. "It is really terribly exciting having him here," Lanny tells Lucy. "It is like having someone out of the distant past step into the present." He adds: "I have thought just seeing him would be the answer to a million questions I have had about who I am and about our whole family." For Lanny, the Senator is the archetypal Southern gentleman— "something you will never see duplicated, never repeated, that there isn't any more of."

III *"By Any Sensible Reckoning of History"*

It is just because the Senator has such significance for Lanny that he becomes an important element in the main drama of the play—a drama which is played out on the unlikely stage of Lanny's sensitive adolescent consciousness. Ultimately, all the external action of the play is related to the maturation process which takes place in Lanny. Lanny is introduced in Act I as a mildly precocious, slightly spoiled, and highly imaginative youth who is seeking his identity in the South's mythic past, which the old Senator symbolizes. Though he begs the Senator to tell him about "the old days back in Tennessee," he is probing for "ideas," not just "stories and anecdotes" like those he hears from his family. The stories may mean something Lanny admits, but he does not know what it is; the Senator does not *have* the answer, Lanny feels, but actually *is* the answer to the riddle of what the stories mean. Lanny has sought answers in history before (his reading ironically includes *The Decline and Fall of the Roman Empire* and a biography of Sam Davis, boy-hero of the Confederacy), but his first exposure to some facts of recent history (the truth about Lucy's relationship to his Uncle William) is so traumatic that it leads to his suicide attempt. Only at the end of the play, when he finally gets his audience with Senator Caswell, does Lanny learn the inadequacy of the past to explain the present.

The climactic revelation occurs in one of the longest speeches of the play, when the Senator, who has previously rebuffed Lanny's inquiries, provides him with the "philosophic point" he has been after. The point is couched in a fable which the Senator narrates about his own similar search for meaning in the experience of another seer-figure, an ancient Negro slave, the son of a Congo chieftain. The then young Cameron Caswell had vicariously lived through old Prince's jungle exploits so vividly that he passionately shared his tribal loyalties, lay awake nights wishing he could have been born to such a life, and had "senseless longings to go to some faraway place and live the life of the noble savage." The relationship, however, is only partly parallel to the present one between Lanny and the Senator, as the Senator explains to Lanny:

> . . . But, you know, even as a little fellow I knew somehow that when I held converse with Prince it was not with a man who had been a boy a hundred years back but, as far as I was concerned, a thousand years back, perhaps ten thousand years. That was something self-evident; there was no confusion in our minds about it . . . (*standing*) But, you see, that would not have been so with you and me. I would have talked to you about old times back home as though it was all day before yesterday, as you no

> doubt believe it was. But it isn't so! By any sensible reckoning of history there are a thousand years between your generation and mine. (*Begins to leave*) Son, a man who was born in 1854 is older than any of the persons assembled in this house tonight has yet dared to dream. And in another decade or two, even such a meeting as that one I addressed tonight—if anyone recalls it—will seem like something out of an age ancient and remote. (158)

That Lanny learns the lesson the Senator teaches is shown by the final gesture of the play. Allowed at last to celebrate his birthday, after the departure of the Senator, Lanny is hesitating over the candles on his birthday cake, wondering what to wish. Goaded by his parents to blow out the candles before he sets the house on fire, Lanny slowly and hypnotically utters the play's curtain line: "Give me time. Give me time." It is his symbolic abandonment of the mythic past for the ever-burning present.

IV *"Nothing in Common but Games"*

Surrounding Lanny throughout the play are the other members of the household who provide parallels with and contrasts to the main action. Each has made or is making some kind of accommodation to the problem Lanny is only now broaching. The Senator, of course, made his long ago. So, too, did Auntie Bet and Flo Dear, who learned to play the only "cards" they had to play. James and Helen have adopted the roles of "eternal sweethearts"; "Their motto," William says, "is: Life must *seem* beautiful." Still wavering in their positions are William and Lucy, and Jim and Nancy.

The point of reference for all is the position of James and Helen, the position most like the traditional. By the device of having one character symbolically assume another character's earlier position, Peter Taylor points out the interrelationships between all the positions. At several moments in the play, it is made clear that William is a modern parallel to the old Senator and that Jim is trying to parallel William. Lucy, moreover, is shown to have the possibility of paralleling either Auntie Bet as a self-willed and independent woman or Helen as an indispensable wife and mother; and Nancy hesitates between Lucy's and Helen's footsteps. The last two analogies are helped by the thoroughly theatrical trick of having both Lucy and Nancy borrow Helen's clothes: Nancy, because she needs an old-fashioned dress for a 1920's party; Lucy, because she has to substitute at the last minute (after Lanny's debacle with the sleeping pills) at the Tennessee Society banquet.

The whole of Act III is little more than a development of Lucy's alternatives. The scene opens with Lucy stopping the pendulum on the mantle clock and ends with her starting it again. In the timeless interval, Lucy hears her possibilities outlined by William and Auntie Bet. William, who has been planning to run out on Lucy, mistakes her in Helen's dress for the wifely Helen and is moved to offer to marry her so they may offer Lanny a new kind of parental relationship. Then Auntie Bet reveals with merciless candor that the alternative to becoming Helen is becoming a loveless nothing. It is significant that, in Act IV, Nancy, who had talked of running away with Jim and/or William, stays behind in Helen's dress; but Lucy "clears out," even tearing Helen's borrowed dress in her haste to get out of it.

Differing attitudes toward the function of a "family" underlie the diverse actions. For William (and for Lucy, too, when she was younger), the family represented a "drag" on one's independence that had to be shaken off; thus they set up their unorthodox liaison supposedly without the hated bindings of "human ties." But, as William says, Lucy "matured"; and he did not. "You know, and I know," William tells her, "it was coming here and seeing James and Helen with their boys that changed you. You began to think maybe farms were not the only place families still made sense. Families were not such awful, out-of-date things, after all. You never said those things, but I could tell when you began to think them." Auntie Bet, whose rich father was never able to find her a husband, kept her life from being "a pretty sad and pointless affair" first by learning to live as the men of her generation did, then by giving up her independence to attach herself to her surrogate children, the Tolliver boys. Nancy and Jim at first wish to escape from family life, but finally, like Lucy, seem to have a change of heart.

Ironically, the exemplars of family responsibility, James and Helen, run a ménage characterized by luxurious extravagance, complete apathy in discipline, and gratuitous indulgence of self and children. The symbolic representation of the ceremonial formality which maintains the facade about them is found in the constantly recurring imagery of games in both the action and the dialogue. The play opens in the game room with Auntie Bet and Flo Dear working a jigsaw puzzle; it closes in the same room with the whole family playing a guessing game over the birthday and anniversary presents. In between, various characters (usually at the instigation of Helen, the perpetual "organizer" of family games) have engaged in gambling contests, crossword puzzles, solitaire, darts, and keno. Helen at one point admits that the games are a deliberate diversion to avoid unwanted thoughts.[8] "The trouble with Mother and Father," Lanny says, "is that they have nothing in common but games. They have to play games to keep from boring each other to death."

The charm of a game is that, involving as it does both luck and skill, it is (in Senator Caswell's words) "like a small abstraction of life itself—so much so that it seems almost a sacred thing." The long discussion of gambling by the various characters in Act II provides the clue for understanding Lanny's suicide attempt, which is taking place at that very moment offstage, following his discovery of William and Lucy's relationship. William argues that "gambling doesn't appeal to people . . . who have real self-confidence or to people who know—or think they know—what life is worth to them," but only to nervous, senseless men who only know "that they have nothing and they ought to want something."

The Senator, on the other hand, admires the gentleman-gamblers of Andrew Jackson's day who felt that gambling was "good for the soul." He emphasizes the part played by luck even in a political campaign: "Campaign all you will, the outcome of an election depends on things too diverse to consider. Everything from the conversion of St. Paul to the defeat of Prince Charlie counts for or against you in one way or another. Everything from the price of rice in China to the price of shoes in St. Louis. How these things fall together for you constitutes your luck" (89). William rejects, however, history's importance to the fortunes of an individual: "You can have history. The trick is to operate outside history. The only interest anybody should have in past history should be for the purpose of better exploiting present history." And this, of course, is very close to the insight which comes to Lanny at the end of the play.

V *"A Stand in the Mountains"*

Eleven years elapsed before Taylor published his next play, *A Stand in the Mountains,* in a special regional theater issue of *Kenyon Review.*[9] Originally called *The Girl From Forkèd Deer,* the play had been gestating for years and had been much revised and expanded just days before its initial publication. *A Stand in the Mountains* is set at Owl Mountain, an imaginary Cumberland Mountain resort for which Taylor has invented a detailed Faulkner-type history, printed in a preface to the play. The main characters are Taylor's usual wealthy urban Southerners, known on Owl Mountain as "the summer people." But there are also two characters representing a type not found in other Taylor works: the primitive, racially mixed mountaineers who have eked out impoverished existences on the depleted plateaus for some two hundred years.

As in *Tennessee Day,* the play opens on a festive occasion, the Fourth of July, the opening of the resort season. Louisa Weaver, the socially prominent widow of a rich Louisville lawyer, has returned to her Owl Mountain cottage with her retinue in tow. The entourage includes her aging but devoted brother-in-law, Will Weaver; a young country cousin, Mina, whom she hopes to introduce to Louisville society in the fall; and, much to her own surprise, her twenty-eight-year-old son Zack, a poet, who has just turned up at home after a rebellious sojourn in Italy. Already at Owl Mountain is Louisa's elder son, Harry, who "in defiance of Louisa's wishes and her strong will" had at an early age married a mountain girl and embraced atavistically the primitive life of the mountaineers. These are joined later by Georgia Morris, a former protégée of Louisa's who ran away in the middle of her debutante season and who is now the wife of an Italian nobleman and the mistress of Louisa's son Zack.

In the seven scenes which constitute the play, complications come quickly. Zack falls in love with Mina, who is already in love with Harry; and Harry falls in love with Georgia. By the end of Scene III, Harry has shot and wounded his mountain wife, Lucille; by the end of Scene V, he has fatally broken her neck; by the end of Scene VI, he has shot and killed his wife's grandmother, his two sons, and himself. Though it is all offstage, there is more intrigue and violent action in this play than in any other of Taylor's works.

Unfortunately, the dramatic climax seems only loosely related to the essential conflicts of the play, which all involve the ambivalent relationships of the other characters to Louisa, who is simultaneously as charming and exasperating as Chekhov's Madame Ranevsky of *The Cherry Orchard.* Harry and Zack are both emasculated boys still trying to "take revenge" on the mother who would have made "male debutantes" out of them; even Uncle Will admits that his long ardor for Louisa has been that of an anxious child for its mother. All three men react to the other women, including Louisa's offstage stepdaughters whom Zack habitually refers to as "Goneril and Regan," as if they were only mirrored aspects of Louisa. "What is it they have all done to us?" Zack asks, alluding to "the female conspiracy." "Let's go into the ladies now," Harry says a little later; "Let's face the real enemy." By turning respectively to history, to poetry, and to atavistic flight, Will, Zack, and Harry attempt to escape woman's ineluctable purpose of ruling men.

At the heart of this conflict are some of the same concerns about women's roles that figured in *Tennessee Day.* Louisa has come from one kind of milieu, the Southern country town; and she has found herself without a clear role in her new milieu, the affluent urban high society. Her preoccupation with the American debutante "institution" is her effort to define her own status. The country cousins she perennially presents to society are, in Mina's words, "her link between Forkèd Deer and Louisville, between the world she came out of and the world she lives in." Louisa has had to make "the best out of all the possibilities her life offered," and her efforts have sometimes been misguided. "To most people she seems the epitome of femaleness," Harry says. "Yet underneath she operates like a man." Later, Harry explains further: "She doesn't know that American women are becoming men and men are becoming women. She doesn't know there is no such thing as a woman's world and a man's world nowadays. She doesn't know what a blur the whole world has become."

Louisa, Georgia, and Mina are all attempting to accommodate themselves to this blurry world, just as Auntie Bet, Lucy, and Nancy were in *Tennessee Day;* and there are striking parallels between the sets of characters—both male and female—in the two plays. It is only when Lucille, the symbol of primitive woman, also becomes demanding and determined to seek her own "advantages" in the manner of Louisa or Mina, that Harry goes on his berserk rampage. This is Harry's form of what Zack calls a new masculine "religion": "You've got to be willing to cut loose, no matter what you get yourself into—cut loose from your own innocent, little children even, if your life requires it." The alternative, as the drunken "oinking" of the three men at the end of Scene IV makes clear, is to become swine in some Circe's pen.

In addition to this central concern, *A Stand in the Mountains* incidentally treats many other provocative themes—the failure of the cities as centers of power and culture, the erosion of place distinctions so that "all places are alike," the quasi-religious aspects of the debutante system, the loss of "the old America," and the lure of the native clay. Whatever defects the play may have come not from a paucity of dramatic ideas but from a failure to provide adequate external correlatives for the interior attitudes which are the real subject. Too many of the characters and subplot complications seem superfluous, dragged awkwardly to illustrate tangential motifs that Taylor could not bring himself to discard, however destructive they were to dramatic cohesiveness. Even more than Taylor's other two plays, *A Stand in the Mountains* suffers from the loss of the chief strength of his fiction—the unifying presence of a narrative consciousness.

CHAPTER 6

Happy Families Are All Alike

I "About Being an Artist"

IT IS ALMOST taken for granted today that the "really serious" creative writer will spend at least half of his time explaining the theories behind the fiction, poetry, or drama he produces in the other half of his time. If the writer is attached to an academic institution or to a literary magazine, his public can expect to find his esthetics set forth in an unending spate of articles, interviews, lectures, letters, and reviews. No matter how voluminous, all this formal theorizing is, of course, merely a gloss on the artistic principles already explicitly articulated in the author's many supposedly imaginative works: stories, plays, and poems dealing interminably with the artist as idealist, the artist as iconoclast, the artist as (alas!) *isolato.*

Peter Taylor does not fulfill these modern expectations. Though he has been a teacher of creative writing at half a dozen colleges and universities, though he has been an advisory editor of a distinguished quarterly (the *Kenyon Review*), though he has been called on to lecture at home and abroad, he has never published any theory or criticism. He has, moreover, generally eschewed in his fiction the subject of art and artists, neither treating it openly (like Joyce or Proust) or hiding it under an allegorical disguise (like Kafka or Tennessee Williams). For this reason, "1939," the one story in which Taylor does take up the subject of art, gains a special importance in the overall study of his work.[1]

"1939," which first appeared in the *New Yorker* in March, 1955, is the first story Peter Taylor published after *The Widows of Thornton;* and in many ways it marks the beginning of a shift in style and format that becomes evident in nearly all the stories in *Happy Families Are All Alike*, his third collection, which came out in 1959. The fact that it deals with the literary aspirations of a young writer much like Peter Taylor in his Kenyon College days helps to provide some clues to the implications of the new direction in his fiction.

The heroes of "1939" are two modern knights-errant on a semimystic quest. That their point of origin is Gambier, Ohio, and their destination New York City, does not diminish the significance of their "ride through the dark, wooded countryside of Pennsylvania on that autumn night" over roads that "wound about the great domelike hills of that region and through the deep valleys in a way that answered some need." For, like their medieval counterparts, these two Kenyon College knights are spurred by an ideal. The narrator confides: "At the time—that is, during the dark hours of the drive East—each of us carried in his mind an image of the girl who had inspired him to make this journey." Furthermore, he recognizes that "the two glorious girls" are but the "particular objects" toward which they are being led by their "inner yearnings for mature and adult experience," the quixotic illusion which they pursue.

The background of the two young men is carefully sketched into the story. The narrator and his roommate, Jim Prewitt, are "restless and uneasy" in the doldrums of their senior year (which, of course, was a tense pre-war year), and they take off on their Thanksgiving holiday jaunt not even sure (they say) that they will return. What they are leaving behind is Douglass House, an old home converted into a residence for a group of student writers, each of whom had transferred to Kenyon College in his sophomore year to study under a "famous and distinguished" poet just appointed to the staff of the English Department. But the two travelers do not think of themselves as linked in any kind of "fraternity" to their fellow students in Douglass House; rather, all the Douglass House inmates see themselves as "independents" who intend to remain independent.

And what of the modern Glorianas they are seeking in New York City? The "two glorious girls" are to the two questing boys both artists themselves and symbols of all that is good in the artistic way of life. Unfortunately, as many a knight has learned before, first impressions can be deceiving. The narrator's artist girl friend, Nancy Gibault, turns out to be neither an artist nor a girl friend. Art school has made her see that she is no artist, and a big bourgeois "German oaf" from St. Louis has made her see she cannot be the narrator's girl friend. In anger and humiliation, the narrator cruelly chides her about her near mistake "about being an artist," saying he could tell at sight that she was not one. Jim Prewitt's girl, on the other hand, is at the other extreme—the extreme of bohemian pretentiousness. Both are lacking in "the talent and the character and the original mind" which the two boys thought they remembered in them; both are as "worldly and as commonplace as could be."

If the two distressing damsels do not provide the noble adventure their cavaliers had expected, they nevertheless are catalysts for a genuinely "mature and adult experience" which leads to the "complete and permanent disenchantment" of the two boys. The climactic event of the journey occurs on the train trip back to Kenyon when the aggrieved young men engage in an almost ceremonial unmasking and combat. As each produces the piece of writing he has just made about his New York experience, the other sarcastically exposes it for what it is: in Jim Prewitt's case, a pompous imitation of W. B. Yeats; in the narrator's case, an unconscious parody of Henry James. There then follows, in the smoking car of the train, a semi-violent joust in which they ram each other with shoulder blocks as though in a "game" of football. Because each recognizes himself in the other, their "mutual abhorrence and revulsion toward any kind of physical contact" between them is so great that neither feels any "impulse to strike the other with his fist or to take hold and wrestle." When they are finally separated by the conductor, the narrator falls into a "blissful" but restless sleep in his coach seat. "Each time, as I dropped off to sleep again," he says, "I would say to myself what a fine sort of sleep it was, and each time it seemed that the wheels of the train were saying: *Not yet, not yet, not yet.*"

One final incident remains in the story. When the now-reconciled travelers reach their room in Douglass House, they find the seven students they left behind gathered for a one o'clock in the morning snack around the narrator's hot plate on the "little three-legged oak table in the very center of the room." At first outraged, the two boys eventually relax, laugh, and join with the others in what amounts to a symbolic fellowship feast about the fraternal Round Table. The youthful would-be artists have apparently learned one adult truth: the artist cannot cut himself off from his fellows in his search for his ideal. But, as the narrator stands groggily surveying the situation, he finds it hard to believe "that the trip was over"; and, as if in confirmation that it is not, he hears again "the train wheels saying *Not yet, not yet, not yet.*"

II *"Mature and Adult Experience"*

The story "1939" focuses attention on two elements which dominate the stories in *Happy Families Are All Alike*. The first is a thematic motif about the relationship of experience to wisdom. The second is a narrative technique which shapes the action into the form of an autobiographical memoir. The experience-wisdom theme is tied to the problem of the artistic quest in "1939." The two Kenyon seniors are vividly convinced as they begin their New York trip that prospective writers have a special responsibility to drink deep of the Pierian Spring:

> The two of us were setting out on this trip not in search of the kind of quick success in the world that had so degraded our former friend [who won a publisher's advance and fled Kenyon] in our eyes; we sought, rather, a taste—or foretaste—of "life's deeper and more real experience," the kind that dormitory life seemed to deprive us of. We expressed these yearnings in just those words that I have put in quotation marks, not feeling the need for any show of delicate restraint. We, at twenty, had no abhorrence of raw ideas or explicit statement. We didn't hesitate to say what we wanted to be and what we felt we must have in order to become that. We wanted to be writers, and we knew well enough that before we could write we had to have "mature and adult experience." And, by God, we *said* so to each other, there in the car as we sped through towns like Turtle Creek and Greensburg and Acme. (219-20)

As the questing pair set off, however, the narrator has a sudden mental glimpse of the Douglass House boys staring after them in which he disconcertingly imagines his own face and that of Jim Prewitt among the gaping figures. "It seemed to me that we had been staring after ourselves with the same fixed, brooding expression in our eyes that I saw in the eyes of the other boys," the narrator says. The implication is that the romantic pursuit of wisdom is a consciously indulged illusion.

The little-boy type of surly self-sufficiency which the narrator affects is contrasted with a more mature type of independence which his girl Nancy gains for herself. Her new autonomy is revealed in her rejection of "the seedy-looking undergraduate in search of 'mature experience'" who is the narrator. "Nancy had never seen me out of St. Louis before, and since she had seen me last, she had seen Manhattan," the narrator realizes. "To be fair to her, though, she had seen something more important than that. She had, for better or for worse, seen herself." To see one's self, the whole story seems to say, is the first step toward wisdom—for the artist as well as for the rest of the world.

Thus it is of great importance to the success of the story that the action is related "in the form of a memoir" from the perspective of the present time. The narrator may not have had great wisdom at the time when he was a participant in the quixotic quest, but somewhere between then and now he has learned to see himself. At one point in the story, after a couple of apparently irrelevant anecdotes, the narrator calls attention to his present point of view:

> Probably I seem to be saying too much about things that I understood only long after the events of my story. But the need for the above digression seemed no less urgent to me than did that concerning the former owner of our car. In his case, the digression dealt mostly with events of a slightly earlier time. Here it has dealt with a wisdom acquired at a much later time. And now I find that I am still not quite finished with speaking of that later time and wisdom. Before seeing me again in the car that November night in 1939, picture me for just a moment—much changed in appearance and looking at you through gold-rimmed spectacles—behind the lectern in a classroom. I stand before the class as a kind of journeyman writer, a type of whom Trollope might have approved, but one who has known neither the financial success of the facile Harvard boy nor the reputation of Carol Crawford. Yet this man behind the lectern is a man who seems happy in the knowledge that he knows—or thinks he knows—what he is about. And from behind his lectern he is saying that any story that is written in the form of a memoir should give offense to no one, because before a writer can make a person he has known fit into such a story—or any story, for that matter—he must do more than change the real name of that person. He must inevitably do such violence to that person's character that the so-called original is forever lost to the story. (222)

This passage makes several points relevant not only to the technique of "1939" but to that of much of Taylor's later work.

In the first place, we can observe that the "memoir" form referred to becomes increasingly popular with Peter Taylor in the stories written after 1955. Although *A Woman of Means* was a first-person narrative, only three of the seven stories in *A Long Fourth* were told in the first person, and not one of the stories in *The Widows of Thornton* was. On the other hand, twelve of the nineteen stories published between 1955 and 1965 are first-person narratives. Furthermore, in these later stories, the biographical facts about the narrators are frequently closely parallel to those of the author himself.

"1939" probably raises the question of autobiography in Peter Taylor's art as pointedly as any other story. Surface details would seem to identify author with character: both were Kenyon seniors in 1939, both had transferred in the sophomore year to study under a famous poet (Taylor following John Crowe Ransom from Vanderbilt), both came from St. Louis (though Taylor more immediately from Memphis), both were close friends of an aspiring poet from Boston (in Taylor's case, Robert Lowell), both later became teachers of creative writing in colleges. Morgan Blum, in his study of Peter Taylor's use of the autobiographical as a type of self-limitation,[2] has pointed out two significant ways in which Taylor has varied autobiographical fact in the story. In the first place, Taylor stresses the narrator's independence and contempt for fraternities, while Taylor himself had once been a member of a major national fraternity. Second, Taylor represents his narrator as being "an insecure and unpublished imitator of Henry James," while he himself in 1939 had already had published two stories and had written at least two more that were subsequently to be published in *Southern Review* and *A Long Fourth.* Other discrepancies, including that fact that the narrator is only twenty in 1939 while Taylor himself was twenty-two, might also be noted. The point in question, Morgan Blum says, is not whether Taylor ever goes beyond the autobiographical (for it is obvious that he does), but "whether he is *ever* autobiographical."

The answer, of course, is that even in the stories that *seem* most autobiographical, Taylor transcends the autobiographical limitation. Taylor has limited himself to the autobiographical, Blum argues, only in the sense that his fictional world is "always a world he has observed, peopled with folk he has observed," never containing a time, an area, or an activity he could not have observed.[3] The memoir form of "1939," then, is only superficially like autobiography; for it has its real-life basis transformed by the shaping vision of the fiction writer.

III "*Ideas and Truth and Work and People*"

Both the experience-wisdom theme and the memoir technique of "1939" can be further elucidated by other stories in *Happy Families Are All Alike*. The experience-wisdom theme, for instance, can be clearly seen in stories like "Promise of Rain" and "*Je Suis Perdu.*"

"Promise of Rain" is the story of wisdom coming to a seemingly mature man of fifty through an unexpected sharing of the vision of his teenage son. The father, Will Perkins, who is also the narrator of the story, summarizes the experience in the last paragraph:

> . . . I had a strange experience that afternoon. I was fifty, but suddenly I felt very young again. As I wandered through the house I kept thinking of how everything must look to Hugh, of what his life was going to be like, and of just what he would be like when he got to be my age. It all seemed very clear to me, and I understood how right it was for him. And because it seemed so clear I realized that the time had come when I could forgive my son the difference there had always been between our two natures. I was fifty, but I had just discovered what it means to see the world through another man's eyes. It is a discovery you are lucky to make at any age, and one that is no less marvelous whether you make it at fifty or fifteen. Because it is only then that the world, as you have seen it through your own eyes, will begin to tell you things about yourself. (68-69)

What would be mere sententiousness out of context becomes a vivid truth as the culmination of a series of events in the story.

How has the father been led to his discovery? The story begins with the father's keeping a highly critical watch on his sixteen-year-old son Hugh, who is most often seen preening himself in front of mirrors when at home or wandering aimlessly about when out on the town with his gang of teenage friends. When Hugh develops through a speech class an interest in his own voice, too, and begins recording himself on an old Dictaphone, the father becomes a little worried by what seems to be the growing vanity of his son's life—vanity both in the sense of narcissism and in the sense of futility. So at a loss is the father in understanding his son that he feels as if he and his son drift "through two different cities . . . laid out on the very same tract of land" and occupy "two different houses built upon one piece of ground —houses of identical dimensions and filling one and the same area of space."

Taylor makes clear, however, through the mirror and Dictaphone imagery, that the boy is only trying to discover himself, to see and hear himself in various roles until he hits upon his true vocation. The father, too, comes to understand this in the crucial incident of the story, the occasion when the boy has a chance to hear himself on radio. The radio station has agreed to carry a public-service program featuring the local speech class only if the regularly scheduled ballgame is rained out that day. Hugh is forced to hope for rain, but the rain which comes and cancels the ballgame also creates such static that the radio program is all but obliterated. The "promise of rain," therefore, is a threat as well. (Several times it is pointed out in the story that Hugh is saving things for a "rainy day.")

On this day of mixed blessings, the father, developing an empathy for his son as they wait out the weather, finally manages to sense what his son is seeking and seeing. And, despite the static in the air, the father knows Hugh has found himself in his desire to go into show business—a desire that the sound of his own voice on the radio-waves confirms once and for all. Having seen the world through another's eyes for that little moment, the father also sees himself in a new light as part of that world. At fifty, he has at last moved toward an essential new wisdom.

The story "*Je Suis Perdu*" provides another illustration of the experience-wisdom theme, again in a father-child relationship. This time the father is younger—thirty-eight—and the child is a little girl of seven. The setting is Paris on the last day of the father's one-year research leave in that city; the father has finished the work which he had hoped to get done on a book, and the family is packing to return to America. In the course of this day's events the father passes through various moods which culminate in an intellectual revelation.

Though the story is divided into two titled sections, "*L'Allegro*" and "*Il Penseroso*," it is more than a Miltonic mood piece. "*Je Suis Perdu*" succeeds because it not only graphically represents complex emotional states but because it also lets us see a character taking an important step toward the philosophic serenity which only genuine maturity can produce. The father begins his day hearing the sound of laughter: the domestic merriment of his wife, their baby son, and their little girl. The mirth is contagious, and the father dwells on all the lucky breaks and happy events of the sabbatical year. The mood is broken only temporarily when the excited little girl accidentally overturns a glass of milk, is scolded by her parents, and trembles out her apology in her newly learned French: "*Je regrette. Je regrette.*" The father then thinks of another recent incident when he had heard another pitiable French cry from his daughter momentarily lost in a movie theater: "*Je suis perdue! Je suis perdue!*"

The memory of this lamentation lingers with the father as he goes for a walk in the Luxembourg Gardens. The despairing cry becomes his own in a way which he cannot at first understand. Looking about him for something outside himself that could have crushed his earlier fine spirits, he at last senses that the melancholy, both loathed and divine, comes from within himself:

> It sprang from the same thing his earlier cheerful mood had come from—his own consciousness of how well everything had gone for him this year, and last year, and always, really. It was precisely this, he told himself, that depressed him. . . . Generally speaking, he didn't dislike being himself or being American, but to recognize that he was so definitely the man he was, so definitely the combination he was, and that certain experiences and accomplishments were now typical of him was to recognize how he was getting along in the world and how the time was moving by. He was only thirty-eight. But the bad thought was that he was no longer *going to be* this or that. He *was.* It was a matter of *be*ing. And to *be* meant, or seemed to mean at such a moment, to *be over with.* (262-63)

Though he recognizes the thought as literary and platitudinous, he is still under its power until he meets his children and their French maid in the park.

The little girl, with her bright blue eyes, is all that is needed to dispel his dark mood. The public buildings are monstrous and tomblike, the park itself is like a formal cemetery, everything about him seems "finished and over with," and his own future life appears "anticlimactic," until the little girl with her "mysterious power" interrupts the mood of despondency. At that point, he realizes that the pensive melancholy will no longer have the hold over him it has had in the past, that he has reached the point where (in Milton's words) "old experience" has attained "to something like prophetic strain." He knows he has gotten to Paris too late to be much affected by his experience (the way, for instance, his little daughter is affected even in her language), but he also knows that what he has already become is also worthwhile. He may be bound now by his own established habits and the claims of others, but he can admit that "there were ideas and truths and work and people that he loved better even than himself."

IV *"Written in the Form of a Memoir"*

"Promise of Rain" is a first-person narrative, *"Je Suis Perdu"* a third-person account. Like most of the other stories in *Happy Families Are All Alike,* they share many qualities of the memoir form alluded to in "1939," despite their variation in point of view. Though the memoir-type story is most likely to be a first-person account, not every first-person tale is in memoir form. An obvious example is the little oddity, "A Walled Garden," which Peter Taylor for some reason chose to include in *Happy Families Are All Alike* after twice passing it up when making his earlier collections.

"A Walled Garden" is certainly first-person in point of view, but it is as far removed from memoir stories like "1939" and "Promise of Rain" as it is possible to be. The form here is rather that of the dramatic monologue of Browning and Tennyson; the story reads, in fact, like a prose parody of Browning's "My Last Duchess." The speaker is a Memphis matron as ruthless and proud as Browning's Duke of Ferrara; her victim is her own daughter, whose behavior, like that of the Duchess, was unpleasing to the speaker. The audience in this case is a young gentleman caller interested in the daughter. The mother, amidst objective appraisals of the flowers in her garden, reminiscent of the Duke's comments on his art collection, gradually reveals to the young man how she has created the magnificent formal garden out of her daughter's former playground. The walled garden, then, becomes a rather obvious symbol for the prison the mother has built about the spirit of the girl.

When first published as "Like the Sad Heart of Ruth" in 1941, "A Walled Garden" might have been excused as a kind of technical experiment which a young writer needed to attempt. Kenneth Clay Cathey has noted that the story has "a tightness of structure and an avoidance of digressions which actually seem to threaten the artistic value of the work."[4] Morgan Blum has been even more blunt: "For me the story has a quality not unlike the one Mr. T. S. Eliot ascribes to the 'anthology piece' in poetry: I find its technical skill a source of real delight, but if it were the only thing of Mr. Taylor's I had read, I cannot believe that I would have gone to any trouble to know more of the author or his remaining writings."[5] In *Happy Families Are All Alike,* "A Walled Garden" probably seems even less impressive by comparison to the more leisurely memoir stories which are Taylor's forte.

If the first-person point of view alone is not enough to make a memoir story, what, then, is necessary? A couple of the more effective stories of this type, "A Friend and Protector" and "The Little Cousins," will illustrate the features that are usually dominant. Both of these stories, first of all, are characterized by a simplicity of style that is highly deceptive. The style is not so much conversational (the way Eudora Welty's is in *The Ponder Heart*) or oratorical (the way Faulkner's is in *Absalom! Absalom!*) or legend-making (the way Carson McCullers' is in "The Ballad of the Sad Café"), as it is—almost—journalistic (the way Robert Penn Warren's might seem to be in *All the King's Men*). It is almost as if the narrator is writing one of those newspaper columns, à la Hal Boyle or Bob Considine, which indulges in folksy reminiscence. We may cite, for examples, the opening lines of "A Friend and Protector" and then of "The Little Cousins":

> Family friends would always say how devoted Jesse Munroe was to my uncle. And Jesse himself would tell me sometimes what he would do to anybody who harmed a hair on "that white gentleman's head." . . . While he was telling me the things he would do, I'd often burst out laughing at the very thought of my uncle's baldness. . . . (113)

> To the annual Veiled Prophet's Ball children were not cordially invited. High up in the balcony, along with servants and poor relations, they were tolerated. . . . But, generally speaking, children were expected to enjoy the Prophet's parade the night before and be content to go to bed without complaint on the night of the Ball. This was twenty-five years ago, of course. There is no

> telling what the practices are out there in St. Louis now. Children have it much better everywhere nowadays. Perhaps they flock to the Veiled Prophet's Ball by the hundred, and even go to the Statler Hotel for breakfast afterward. (148)

The tone is familiar but not really personalized, friendly but not intimate, subjective but not very confidential. It neither promises nor delivers anything that might not be publicly discussed in print if the account were autobiographical and not fictional.

The memoir story is, more importantly, retrospective. The main events are never in the immediate present, but are far enough removed in time to be viewed somewhat dispassionately and, perhaps, with an understanding derived from the perspective in time. Stories like "The Scoutmaster" and *A Woman of Means* show that Taylor knew and used the retrospective approach early in his career with great success. In the stories in *Happy Families Are All Alike*, the temporal distance between happening and narration is nearly always pointed out. In both "A Friend and Protector" and "The Little Cousins," for instance, we get the impression that the narrator is a man at least in his thirties, but in the one story he is harking back to some events in his late teens and in the other to an episode when he was nine years old. The emphasis in the stories is not, then, what it would have been if the telling had been closer to the event.

Chronology is not even very important in the typical memoir story. The narrator usually feels free to range backward and forward from the time of the principal event (if there is one), with momentary stops at any attractive spot on the temporal spectrum. The transitional words in a single paragraph of "A Friend and Protector" illustrate the pattern: "Usually . . . . And besides by the time I came along . . . . There had been a number of years when . . . . Then, after this phase . . . ." Habitual action receives at least as much stress in this kind of story as the unusual and dramatic kind.

As a result of the de-emphasizing of temporal sequence, the memoir story hardly seems to have a plot in any conventional sense. Its structure appears as loosely anecdotal as, say, a *Reader's Digest* sketch on "The Most Unforgettable Character I Ever Met." A look at the climaxes in "A Friend and Protector" and in "The Little Cousins" shows, however, that the apparent plotlessness is an illusion. In the former story, the narrator looks back on the relationships between his uncle and aunt and their Negro handyman, Jess Munroe. He recalls (though not in sequential order) how Jesse, while back in the country town of Braxton, Tennessee, had "received a suspended sentence for an alleged part in the murder of Aunt Margaret's washwoman's husband," how Uncle Andrew arranged with the judge to bring Jesse with him and Aunt Margaret when they moved to Memphis, how Jesse began to go on escapades and get into scrapes to counteract the "country boy" teasing he got from the other servants, how Uncle Andrew would always get him out of his jams, and how Jesse's drinking and wild (even criminal) ways grew successively worse. Finally, Jesse goes on a drunken rampage in which he wrecks and ravages Uncle Andrew's office. This time, barricading himself in the ruined office, he calls not for Uncle Andrew but Aunt Margaret.

When the old woman faces Jesse through the glass door of the office, the narrator suddenly senses the truth about the "protective" relationship he has witnessed over the years:

> While she remained there her behavior was such that it made me understand for the first time that this was not merely the story of that purplish-black, kinky-headed Jesse's ruined life. It is the story of my aunt's pathetically unruined life, and my uncle's too, and even my own. I mean to say that at this moment I understood that Jesse's outside activities had been not only *his*, but *ours* too. My Uncle Andrew, with his double standard or triple standard—whichever it was—had most certainly forced Jesse's destruction upon him, and Aunt Margaret had made the complete destruction possible and desirable to him with her censorious words and looks. But they did it because they had to, because they were so dissatisfied with the pale *un*ruin of their own lives. They did it because something would not let them ruin their own lives as they wanted and felt a need to do—as I have often felt a need to do, myself. As who does not sometimes feel a need to do? Without knowing it, I think, Aunt Margaret wanted to see Jesse as he was that morning. (136)

This stunning climax, which reverses ironically all the relationships the rest of the story has established, is followed by an anticlimax that is in some ways even more startling. For the narrator finds that Aunt Margaret, far from suffering as he had supposed from a lasting shock, shows no permanent awareness of her role as Jesse's Judas.

In "The Little Cousins," the reminiscences also build up to a nonspectacular but moving denouement. The narrator, recalling his motherless boyhood and the childish sufferings that only his sister Corinna could share and name for him, concludes with what appeared to outsiders as a trivial incident. But the incident is again a betrayal—not as socially destructive as the one in "A Friend and Protector," but just as heartrending to the nine-year-old boy. For years, the boy has relied on the silent pact that binds his sister to him as companion, confidante, and comforter. The strength of the alliance has been a common enemy, Mary Elizabeth Caswell, an older girl, also motherless, who is held up as a paragon of virtue to the two children. At the story's end, the boy finds his sister—overwhelmed by Mary Elizabeth Caswell's glamour and graciousness as Queen of the Veiled Prophet's court—capitulating to the enemy in overtures of friendship. Most devastating of all is the fact that Corinna shares with Mary Elizabeth a special secret which was not hers alone but her brother's as well. So crushed is the little boy by this unexpected abandonment that he bursts into tears which he cannot even explain to the solicitously inquiring adults about him.

The memoir story, then, is different from the non-fictional memoir in the way that any work of imaginative literature is different from the literal reproduction of mere facts: it is the product of a carefully controlled design imposed upon the chaos of life in such a way as to reveal transcendent meaning.

V *Memories, Manners, and Realism*

Peter Taylor's memory for the acutely perceived details of social situations is the sustaining force for all the stories in *Happy Families Are All Alike,* both those that are written in memoir form and those that are not. What Katherine Anne Porter once said of herself—that the "exercise of memory" was the "chief occupation" of her mind—might equally well be applied to Taylor. "All my experience seems to be simply memory, with continuity, marginal notes, constant revision and comparison of one thing with another," Miss Porter has said. "Now and again thousands of memories converge, harmonize, arrange themselves around a central idea in a coherent form, and I write a story."[6]

The result of such a convergence of memories in Peter Taylor's work is a close-webbed texture of social realism in the narrative background—as in the story "Guests," one of the most successful in the 1959 collection. According to an interviewer's report, the first two lines of this story—"The house was not itself. Relatives were visiting from the country."—were written "without any notion of a plot to follow them." Rediscovered by their author five years later, the same lines inspired a new convergence of memories and imagination, and "the story of a do-gooder wife who insists on importing visitors popped into place."[7]

In "Guests," as in many other Taylor stories, the social realism seems to be a compound of three distinct elements: the authentic reproduction of lifelike details in setting, character description, and dialogue; the distillation of an entire code of manners (or, in this instance, of two different codes of manners) into the dramatic conflicts of the plot; and a clear reflection of the psychological reactions occasioned by the code or codes of manners in the particular context.

The first element is readily apparent in "Guests," noticeable especially in the details which contrast the old country couple, Cousin Johnny and Cousin Annie Kincaid, with their big city host and hostess, Edmund and Henrietta Harper. Cousin Johnny's high-topped shoe, his lisle sock held up by an elastic supporter, and his long underwear showing above the sock are part of this authentic representation of life, but so too is Henrietta's stylish dress with the mysterious buttons—"so unnecessary, so numerous and so large"—which are carefully camouflaged by being covered with the same print material the dress is made of. The same kind of realism is found in the perfectly rendered conversations—Edmund is trying to be unperturbed when Henrietta's phone call interrupts a conference with his law partner and his most important client, or Cousin Annie is trying to make a point about how her husband should be addressed (she prefers the "old-fashioned country genteel" form "Mr. Kincaid") while she is actually talking about his distaste for meat.

The second kind of realism—the recreation of the intricate behavioral patterns of characters from different social groups—almost merges with the realism of physical surface. It is only the fact that literary history has produced many Arnold Bennetts but only a few Jane Austens that makes it desirable to keep the two levels separate. Certainly, "Guests" uses surface detail to suggest the different codes of manners of the hosts and the guests: the picture, for instance, of the old country couple "seated side by side on the porch swing—rigid as two pieces of graveyard statuary," all packed and fully dressed, their hats on their heads and their house stoutly locked, waiting for their hosts to pick them up.

But in this story, Peter Taylor has used an even more emphatic means of calling attention to the comedy of manners he is writing; he has filled the story with the imagery of battle, so that the conflict between Cousin Annie's code and Henrietta's becomes hilariously (and, perhaps also, pathetically) clear. Henrietta is determined that her guests shall have their good attended to, their best interests served, willy-nilly; Cousin Annie is determined that they shall endure the outrages of Henrietta's good works without Henrietta's even knowing when or how she offends them. The battle lines are drawn in the opening paragraph:

> Cousin Johnny was on a strict diet. Yet wanting to be no trouble, both he and Cousin Annie refused to reveal any principle of his diet. If he couldn't eat what was being served, he would do without. They made their own beds, washed out their own tubs, avoided using salad forks and butter knives. Upon arriving, they even produced their own old-fashioned ivory napkin rings, and when either of them chanced to spill something on the table cloth, they begged the nearest Negro servant's pardon. As a result, everybody, including the servants, was very uncomfortable from the moment the old couple entered the house. (170-71)

At first, Edmund thinks Cousin Annie is "waging a merely defensive war against Henrietta," but gradually he sees that she has had "the offensive from the beginning" and even wins the final "victory" when Cousin Johnny dies in the guest bedroom without his hosts' ever knowing for sure that he had been ill.[8]

Manners are especially important in the quiet world that Peter Taylor creates, because it is manners that his characters respond to in the moments of heightened perception when they see something anew or for the first time. Thus, in "Guests," what Edmund comes to recognize beneath the social differences is a basic similarity between himself and Cousin Johnny. At first, he finds a part of himself "always reaching out and wanting to communicate" with the country guests and another part "forever holding back, as though afraid of what *would* be communicated." Later, "in a flight of fancy that was utterly novel to him," he visualizes how he himself might have been only a country lawyer and Cousin Johnny might have been a shoe company president if each had followed an earlier opportunity.

And, finally, in a silent soliloquy before Cousin Johnny's corpse, he notes that what they had in common was "being from the country," though each had been in some way dissatisfied and responded to the dissatisfaction in his own way: "... By 'country' we mean the old world, don't we Cousin Johnny—the old ways, the old life, where people had real grandfathers and real children, and where love was something that could endure the light of day —something real, not merely a hand one holds in the dark so that sleep will come. Our trouble was, Cousin Johnny, we were lost without our old realities. We couldn't discover what it is people keep alive for without them ..." (206). The realistic psychological resolution of the story, then, comes naturally from the physical and social realism already established.

Since what appears to be the reality is not always what actually is the reality, a story like "Guests" abounds in little ironies. Thus, Henrietta, who has seemed to be the overwhelming power in the story, turns out vanquished at the hands of her seemingly docile antagonist; and Edmund, who had always accepted Henrietta's contention that she was "more sensitive to people" than he was, turns out to be the only one who senses the full truth of the situation in which they are involved. Although Taylor limits the story to Edmund's point of view, he is still able to unmask fundamental reality by rending its disguises.

In a story like "Heads of Houses," where several points of view are alternately taken up in the story, Taylor is able to multiply a situation's ironies. Perhaps the funniest story Taylor has ever written, "Heads of Houses" is also one of the most serious in theme. Here the three levels of realism are each filtered through three different consciousnesses, so that one viewpoint complements and corrects another.

The subject of "Heads of Houses" is one of those domestic dilemmas that only a few other writers (John Updike is one) even deign to treat anymore. A young couple, Professor Dwight Clark and his wife Kitty, are about to wind up a dutiful summer visit with Kitty's parents, Judge Nathan Parker and Mrs. Parker, at their vacation cottage near Chattanooga. The two "heads of houses" are both happy to see the parting day arrive, but each wishes to conceal his delight from the other and to maintain a shaky facade of friendliness. The comedy of errors begins as each systematically misinterprets the well-intentioned gestures of the other.

Details of the situation are presented first from Dwight's point of view, then from the Judge's, with a reversal in judgment accompanying each shift in viewpoint. Thus Dwight sees himself as speedy and efficient, his little English Ford as sensibleness itself; his father-in-law sees him as "a great clumsy farm animal," his car as an ugly, awkward, disreputable affectation that advertised "how committed Dwight was to whatever it was he thought he was committed to." When Judge Parker inquires about Dwight's gas mileage, he is only trying to distract Dwight from the flowerbeds he is about to stumble into; Dwight, of course, thinks only malevolent sarcasm underlies the awkward question. Nevertheless, the two men, antagonistic as they are on most subjects, can agree on one indisputable fact: that Kitty's old bachelor brother, Henry, is a naïve and bungling incompetent who cannot command respect of the sort due to the head of a house.

Taylor casts a new light on the physical, social, and psychological realities of the situation when he permits us near the conclusion of the story to glimpse Henry's point of view. The Judge and the Professor have been able to see the ways in which they are diametrically opposed; Henry is able to see the underlying similarity between the two. Only Henry knows the separate secrets the two men are hiding—the secret that Dwight is only pretending to have been called back early to his college and the secret that the Judge has already scheduled a party with his friends for right after the young couple's departure. "Each of them was suffering from an acute awareness that he was practicing a stupid deception upon the other, as well as from a fear that he might be discovered." Henry realizes that they relish badgering him as a "common enemy" because they resent his lack of involvement in the domestic trivialities which occupy them.

Certainly Henry is one of the finest and most original characters Peter Taylor has ever created. Though he willingly plays "the role he was assigned" as the uncomplicated and unperceptive old bachelor, Henry actually leads another life (which his relatives must suspect but won't acknowledge) as the futile lover of a married woman whose husband won't give her a divorce. In the precariousness of his own position, Henry cannot muster much sympathy for the two other men, who at least have their own brands of "certainty" to fall back upon. The two heads of houses are comic foils whose problems are lilliputian compared to his. "What was one summer, more or less, of not having things just as you wanted them?" Henry thinks. "Next summer, or even tomorrow, or an hour from now, each of them would have it all his way again." If neither Dwight nor the Judge had found the variety of certainty for which he was ideally suited, each had at least a kind of security in his accepted values that Henry can appreciate better than they.

The revelations at the end of the story ring true because the whole context is accurately drawn from life. From the sight of the basket of fruit that the mother-in-law tries to foist on the departing family to the sound of the old pump about to wheeze out as the children flush and reflush the toilet, the setting is authentic. And Taylor's dialogue has never more efficienctly rendered the background of manners of his speakers. It is no wonder, then, that the human vanities and frustrations manifested amidst such verisimilitude seem to have universal validity.

VI *The Commonplace and the Grotesque*

If there is a formula to the typical Peter Taylor story at this stage of Taylor's career, it should be revealed by a comparison of the two remaining stories in *Happy Families Are All Alike*—"The Other Times" and "Venus, Cupid, Folly and Time." The first story would probably impress a reader conditioned to Peter Taylor's unspectacular techniques as a competent and rewarding enough piece by the kind of "journeyman writer" described in "1939." The other, which was enough of a virtuoso performance of some kind to win an O. Henry Awards first prize, would probably strike the appreciative student of Peter Taylor as a little bit untrue to Taylor's own unique vision.

What makes the difference in the two stories? Superficially, the two pieces are much alike. Each is a first-person narrative by a middle-aged man recalling some events of his adolescence. Each is structured in the Sterne-like digressive-progressive form of the "memoir" story. Each deals with some aspect of the wisdom-experience theme. Moreover, both stories are set in Chatham, the mythical city Peter Taylor has created as "a composite of Columbus, St. Louis, Memphis—all cities in which the author has lived."[9] Chatham is described in "The Other Times" as a "middle-sized city" and "a good place to grow up in," being "not thoroughly Middle Western and yet not thoroughly Southern either," and in "Venus, Cupid, Folly and Time" as a "rather old city" that is considered "geographically Northern and culturally Southern." Although neither of the stories under consideration gives the kind of detailed picture of Chatham as a city which "Promise of Rain" gives, both convey graphic impressions of the ideas and attitudes of the monied class during the years of the Great Depression. Chatham seems of a piece with the St. Louis, Detroit, and Chicago of numerous other Taylor works.

Probably the chief contrast between the two stories is one of mood. "Can anybody honestly like having a high-school civics teacher for an uncle?" the narrator asks in the opening sentence of "The Other Times." The first few paragraphs set up an expectation that this will be another leisurely exploration of familial relationships on the order of "The Scoutsmaster" or "A Wife of Nashville." On the whole, the story does not disappoint this expectation, but it is hardly one of Taylor's most memorable stories. It probes, satisfactorily enough, the mysterious bonds of family love which link a young girl to her uncle in a way in which she will never be linked to the narrator, her high-school beau.

The plot has a trio of senior boys taking their pre-deb dates away from a society party and to a speak-easy roadhouse in a neighboring town. There the narrator and the girl Letitia discover her ne'er-do-well uncle, the civics teacher and baseball coach at Chatham's Westside High School, carousing with some of his athletes and their girl friends. When the place is raided by the authorities, it is Uncle Louis who, after helping hide Letitia and her friends, gallantly sacrifices himself to the humiliation of public arrest (and to the consequent loss of his job). The story ends with the narrator, whose rarefied snobbery pervades the whole account, puzzling over the delicate familial trust that united Letitia with her uncle.

Simple technically but complex thematically, "The Other Times" is a study of the tenuous survival of older patterns in a new cultural climate. Its whole method is understatement: understated characters, understated action, understated themes. "Venus, Cupid, Folly and Time," on the other hand, is one of the few stories in which Peter Taylor abandons the characteristic method of understatement and deliberately distorts his material for a surrealistic shock effect.

The unusual Gothic mood of "Venus, Cupid, Folly and Time" begins with the first sentence: "Their house alone would not have made you think there was anything so awfully wrong with Mr. Dorset or his old maid sister." The "dilapidated and curiously mutilated" house would not make us think there was anything "so awfully wrong," that is, as long as we had not already read Faulkner's "A Rose for Emily," Welty's "Clytie," McCullers' "The Ballad of the Sad Café," Capote's *Other Voices, Other Rooms,* or a hundred and one other contemporary Southern stories with decadent houses for even more decadent people. When the house is more fully described a couple of pages later (it has the third story "torn away" and looks "raw and naked" from the "scars" where a wing was pulled down), the reader should be convinced that something is "awfully wrong" with Peter Taylor's usual style.

The Dorsets are the most grotesque caricatures Taylor has indulged himself with since Mr. Speed in "A Spinster's Tale." We are asked to believe that they are ancient recluses who emerge from their house only three times each year—once to sell artificial flowers (like "sprays of tinted potato chips"), which Miss Dorset makes; once to peddle the withered figs off the family tree; and once (yes, Taylor insists on this, too) to gather up all the pubescent thirteen- and fourteen-year-olds in socially prominent West Vesey Place for a bizarre dancing party at their house. The story is the narrator's account of one of these parties, one where two of the invited children smuggle in an intruder and play a crude trick on the aged host and hostess.

It is perhaps as a result of Peter Taylor's own distrust of this unfamiliar material that he chooses to keep the narrator distant from the main action. The narrator was not even present at the crucial party; he must reconstruct it from the half-legendary accounts of others, filling in details from other related memories. So merged is the description of the one particular party with the recollections of parties of other years that the reader is inclined to accept the narrator's statement that "nothing about the one evening when you were actually there ever seemed quite as real as the glimpses and snatches which you got from those people before and after you—the second-hand impressions of the Dorsets' behavior, of things they said, of looks that passed between them." Even when the events of the climactic occasion have been outlined, the narrator offers little help in interpretation:

> But a clear picture of the whole evening wasn't to be had—not without considerable searching. For one thing, the Meriwether parents immediately, within a week after the party, packed their son and daughter off to boarding schools. Accounts from the other children were contradictory and vague—perversely so, it seemed. Parents reported to each other that the little girls had nightmares which were worse even than those which their older sisters had had. And the boys were secretive and elusive, even with us older boys when we questioned them about what had gone on. (94)

The story is filled with a number of hints that it may be a multi-leveled allegory or at least a richly symbolic oneiric fantasy. The Dorsets are, for instance, despite their eccentricities, the "social arbiters" of the city whose ludicrous demands must be submitted to even by "sensible parents" who might wish to reject them. Are they then figures in a fable about the decline of genteel society? But the Dorsets also seems to visualize themselves as prophets of love, youth, beauty, and sacrifice; "We have given up everything for each other," Miss Dorset says at one time, and adds at another, "This is what it is like to be young forever." And what about the constant insinuations that aberrant sexuality plays a part in their peculiar actions? What about the erotic artwork, slightly hidden and subtly lighted, in the niches and dark corners of their house? What about the color print of Bronzino's "Venus, Cupid, Folly and Time" on the landing of the basement stair? The very subtitle of this picture is "An Allegory"; is that also the implied subtitle of Taylor's story?[10]

The story is too richly suggestive to be easily limited to a single interpretation, and its imaginative resources were no doubt what impressed the judges for both the O. Henry and the Martha Foley short-story annuals.[11] "Venus, Cupid, Folly and Time" is, no doubt, a tour de force, a genuine success of a kind, a worthy contribution to the modern Southern literature of the grotesque. "The Other Times" is only a straightforward realistic chronicle without noticeable distortion for suggestive effect.[12] But "The Other Times" is typical Peter Taylor, and "Venus, Cupid, Folly and Time" is not.

CHAPTER 7

Miss Leonora and *Collected Stories*

I *A Retrospective View*

PETER TAYLOR's two latest volumes, *Miss Leonora When Last Seen* (1963)[1] and *Collected Stories* (1969),[2] both bring together some new stories and reassemble some old ones from earlier out-of-print volumes. They thus provide occasions for a retrospective view of Taylor's past career as well as for an assessment of the scope and direction of his most recent literary efforts.

At the time *Miss Leonora* was compiled in 1963, the two early collections published by Harcourt, Brace, *A Long Fourth* and *The Widows of Thornton*, as well as the novel *A Woman of Means* published by the same firm, had long been out of print. Peter Taylor's prestige, however, was at a relatively high peak. The *Sewanee Review* had, in the fall of 1962, devoted practically an entire issue to the publication of Taylor's story "At the Drugstore" and to three appreciative essays about his writing.[3] Respectful notice was also being given to Taylor in several books of literary history or criticism either recently published or soon to be published.[4] Furthermore, Taylor had just had a Rockefeller Foundation grant added to his list of honors and awards, and he was soon to start a semester's sojourn at Harvard University lecturing on creative writing.

Taylor's new publishers, Ivan Obolensky, Inc., who had published *Happy Families Are All Alike* and who were to take over the rights to *Tennessee Day in St. Louis* from Random House, consequently felt that something like a "Collected Stories" edition was called for. They decided to reprint "his best early stories" along with some previously uncollected ones in the new volume. *Miss Leonora* therefore includes six new stories, four stories from *A Long Fourth,* and five stories and the one-act play from *The Widows of Thornton.* What is most surprising is the choice of stories to be preserved from the early collections.

Some of the selections, of course, reveal Taylor at his very best: stories like "The Fancy Woman" and "A Wife of Nashville" and "What You Hear From 'Em?"—stories that would have been inevitable on anyone's list of favorites. Others, like "Sky Line," "Their Losses," and "Cookie," are also first-rate stories and fairly representative of Taylor's characteristic themes and techniques. The remaining selections, though they are all respectable works, seem included more for the purpose of revealing the versatility of the author than for the purpose of preserving his most distinguished work. *The Death of a Kinsman* was perhaps a forced and not really regrettable choice to display Taylor's playwriting talent. Stories quite untypical of Taylor's ordinary style ("A Spinster's Tale," "Allegiance," "Bad Dreams") may have been reprinted here just to show that Taylor can create grotesque psychological symbols and do some of the other tricks associated with the Gothic school of Southern writing, even if he does not qualify as a full-fledged member of that literary school.

It is not so much that the preserved stories are bad ones; it is only that better ones are crowded out. There are no more accomplished stories in *A Long Fourth* than the three that were passed by: "The Scoutmaster," "Rain in the Heart," and "A Long Fourth." And, in *The Widows of Thornton,* "Two Ladies in Retirement" and "The Dark Walk" are in many ways superior to "Bad Dreams" and, perhaps, even to "Cookie." Yet, as the editors and even Taylor himself must have known, a volume composed of Peter Taylor's very best would have been unbearably repetitious since the very best stories are all of a piece: almost monotonously concerned with the same kind of subject matter, the same kind of themes, and the same kind of techniques.

Versatility certainly is not what distinguishes Peter Taylor's fiction. Like many another young writer,[5] Taylor early in his career tried out a number of forms and techniques and succeeded admirably with several. But he soon learned to direct his talents principally into a narrow channel where he could operate most smoothly. A writer does not write about what he wishes to write about, the late Flannery O'Connor once argued, but about "what he is able to make live."[6] Peter Taylor, as Morgan Blum has pointed out, knows "his own limitations";[7] it is no disgrace that his best work lies inside these limitations.

II *Stretching the Boundaries*

What of the new stories in *Miss Leonora When Last Seen?* Are they only variations on past themes, repetitions of past successes? From one point of view, these six new stories attempt very little that is innovative, even for Taylor; from another, they illustrate what amount and what kind of variety is possible within Taylor's forte. The two stories with which the volume opens, "Reservations: A Love Story" and "An Overwhelming Question," provide contrasting examples of Taylor's attempts to stretch the boundaries which contain what he can "make live." They both deal with young lovers: the first, with a couple on their wedding day; the second, with a couple in the three days before their scheduled wedding. The subject is something new for Taylor, for the nuptial period is the one phase of married life he has hardly touched on since "Rain in the Heart" in 1945 (where, incidentally, his emphasis was on something else).

"Reservations" introduces us to a bride and groom, Franny and Miles, just as they are making their furtive getaway from the lavish wedding reception and supper dance underway at the country club. Trying to elude their prankster friends and to slip off unobserved, the young newlyweds, each led separately by club employees to their escape hatch in the boy's locker room, are practically thrust into each other's arms and impersonally sent off on their own together. The situation is complicated by a snowstorm, which prevents their going to their previously planned honeymoon destination and forces them to spend their wedding night in town.

Taylor very ably portrays the alternating surges of anxiety and of bliss which sweep over the new bride. At first, in the dark locker room, for instance, Franny is convinced that Miles has not shown up, has already deserted her; in the next second, when the maid points him out as right before her, she releases her pent-up emotion, not by rushing to her bridegroom, but by a frenetic farewell hug for the maid. When she gets off the elevator at the hotel, her equilibrium is so upset she nearly faints; but, once they are alone in their room, she becomes again her "vivacious, unaffected, ingenuous" self. These shifts in mood are nothing, however, compared to the drastic changes she undergoes when, at the climax of the story, she accidentally locks herself in the bathroom.

The little bathroom crisis presents the young couple with more than a problem in locksmithery; the unbudging door is a symbol of all the barriers still between them. Taylor has so contrived the situation, too, that Franny and Miles must open the door between them—both the literal and the figurative one—without calling on the usual sources of aid. For the hotel where they are staying is the very hotel where Miles has been living for the last year and a half—the only hotel in the convention-filled city where they were able to get reservations at the last minute when their other plans were canceled by snow. Franny is adamant that Miles shall not call on the hotel employees for help, since the assistant hotel manager is a friend who would not be likely to keep the story of their embarrassment to himself. Miles thus must work on the hinges with jackknife and bottle opener while Franny jiggles the knob.

In the meantime, Franny, in her frustration, and Miles, in his irritation at Franny's locking the door in the first place, begin to raise their voices, to exchange accusations and threats, and to hurt and humiliate one another. All the buried grievances are disinterred—Mile's dallyings with other girls; Franny's family's probing into Miles's background—until Franny threatens to drown herself in the bathtub, and Miles vows to jump out the eighth-floor window if she does. The deus ex machina is an unexpected one: a middle-aged prostitute in the room next door gets her gentleman to extricate Franny through an adjoining door. Ironically, the rescuer, Franny suspects, is none other than the assistant hotel manager they had been trying to avoid!

The crisis is past, and the young lovers are the better off for having weathered it. The "reservations" they have had in their relationship have been canceled:

> In their hearts both of them were glad they had said all the things that they said through the door. As they gazed deep into each other's eyes, they believed that they had got all of that off their chests once and for all. There was nothing in the world to come between them now. They believed, really and truly, that neither of them would ever deceive or mistrust the other again. Silently they were toasting their own bliss and happiness, confident that it would never again be shadowed by the irrelevances of the different circumstances of their upbringings or by the possibly impure and selfish motives that had helped to bring them together. (31)

Though Taylor's tone ironically qualifies the optimism expressed, there at least seems little danger of Franny's earlier despairing vision ("of her dear Miles and her dear self lying dead in their caskets with their love yet unfulfilled") coming true.

The second story, "An Overwhelming Question," is also about the misunderstanding between lovers. The comic situation seems promising enough. Isabel Havens is determined to seduce her fiancé, Rudy Banks, in the three days remaining before their wedding. Her rationale is hilarious:

> She believed still that she had made a mistake in her self-denial; her heart, or her mind, was still set upon remedying her mistake, upon breaking the solemn resolution which some other Isabel, in one of her other lives, had made for her. That was still her fierce, firm purpose, her overwhelming necessity even. And now something strengthened her resolve. As Rudy's smile faded, she saw a look in his eyes that was unbearable to her. . . . She *would not* serve his purpose. She would not allow him to keep the resolution made by another Rudy Banks. She would not, on their wedding night, be there merely as his idealized something or other. (45)

Rudy, though quite a playboy with other women, is just as determined to preserve his "idealized something or other" for his wedding night and so tries to elude Isabel's wiles.

If Peter Taylor in this story relies on the surest suspense plot ever invented, he reserves to himself the right to spring surprises in the denouement. The reader may not know at once just what Taylor is up to, but he should be able to sense at once that "An Overwhelming Question" is a far remove in style and tone from "Reservations." Whereas in "Reservations" the point of view is fairly well restricted to what the young couple sees and feels, either separately or jointly, the point of view in the second story is more objective, with the author commenting directly on his characters as "solemn," for instance, or "comical." Moreover, though there are many realistic observations, in the typical Taylor style, about the manners and mores of the Hunt and Polo Club set, both the central characters and their absurd maneuverings appear amusing but artificial. Franny and Miles seem credible people in a real-life plight; Isabel and Rudy seem highly entertaining characters in a quaint little farce.

But is farce really the explanation? The surprise ending suggests otherwise. Rudy, fleeing again from Isabel's advances, runs out of the new clubhouse, through mud and muck, and onto a junkpile of construction materials, where he slips and falls. "It would be many hours before they found him there, and meanwhile the stars shone on his uncovered head and on the muddy soles of his dress slippers," the impersonal narrator intones. "His neck was broken, the life gone out of his body, but he was safe from Isabel at last, poor fellow."

Though the popularity of the so-called black humorists today makes such a resolution to comic complications familiar to most readers, there is little preceding the denouement to suggest that Peter Taylor is attempting black humor here; the tone, while it is not just Taylor's usual understated irony, is not quite that of a Terry Southern or a Joseph Heller. One is tempted to read the story more closely a second or third time to see if Isabel and Rudy are not perhaps abstractions in some allegory about the battle of the sexes. Yet, if such an interpretation is possible, it is hardly probable; and it certainly is not forced by the details in the story.

The comparison of the two stories, then, suggests that Peter Taylor can break out of his usual limitations by delving into slightly new subject matter. But it also suggests that he is at least as likely to succeed artistically with the new material when he approaches it in his old, accustomed way, as when he attempts a new and uncongenial technique.

III *"A Kind of Knowledge"*

How many times can an author profitably re-cover familiar ground? As long, Peter Taylor might say, as he can perceive new mysteries to explore. The mysteries of human personality, of social interaction, of time and change—these are unfathomable profundities which Taylor's new stories in *Miss Leonora* plumb just a little deeper than they have been plumbed before. The title "A Strange Story," which Taylor gives to one of these new efforts, suggests that just such a mystery will be found at the heart of the narrative.

"A Strange Story" is a first-person account by a middle-aged protagonist of the enigmatic "voices" that plagued him as a little boy. "How are they to be explained, the voices one heard as a child?" he asks in the first line of the story. If the story does not provide a definite answer, it at least provokes thought about the possibilities.

The narrator recalls instance after instance when he distinctly heard "voices that came out of the air, from the trunks of trees, and even sometimes out of the mouths of small anmials." "You are the Lost Dauphin," the voices might say, or "Good morning to you, Bonaparte." Their messages range from the philosophic to the absurd: "Time passes. You haven't got forever"; "Are you going to sit on that Christmas-tree all day?"; "There is no one god. And there was no beginning and there will be no end"; and "Oh, ouch, oh, ouch, ouch, ouch!" The narrator, however, rejects categorically the explanation that he was either an "abnormal child" or a "mystic"; he insists instead that the voices he has heard are heard by all children until they are formally forsworn and replaced by the voices of other people. The narrator is different from others only in that he made the mistake of speaking "frankly" on the subject and embarrassing others, who would react not in "disbelief" but in "disgust" at the breach of good taste.

Mixed with the madcap story of the voices is a realistic story of the narrator's growing up. The crucial incident here is a dancing-class party where the narrator's date is stolen by his older brother. The two stories merge when, in his distress over the events at the party, the narrator repudiates his pestiferous voices and vows, "I will stop hearing you, you demons who persecute innocent children." From that point on, his task is "learning to listen to the voices of people—still discovering just how carefully, for love's sake, one must always listen."

This half-fantastic, half-humorous parable has something more than half-serious to say about human sensibility and human intuition at different stages of maturity. If we are not born trailing Wordsworthian clouds of glory, we may nevertheless be in closer contact with the numinous forces of nature as children than we are as adults. Just as the narrator cannot give to his brother the principles by which he instinctively draws well, so he cannot explain the voices he hears. The unexplained "mystery" of the voices, however, is something to be relished. As the narrator says:

> My liking for the mystery of them has increased with every bit of other learning I have had to do. Such a mystery becomes, finally, a kind of knowledge. It instructs and informs us about the

> arbitrary nature of most of the things we have to learn in order to walk the world as adults. Learn those things we *must,* but we possess the knowledge in our hearts that it might have been different. Our requirement might have been to make sense out of what the voices were saying, and, in that case, those of us whose inclination was to go on listening always to our voices would be the normal ones and not the rare birds we are. (132-33)

Told that he cannot be an artist unless he learns to "love Nature," the narrator eventually learns that "strange and wonderful" feat. But he remains ever aware how far in his mind he has had to "withdraw" from trees and other things of Nature "in order to learn to love them." Love, Peter Taylor seems to say, is a relationship between separate entities; but there is, in children at least, a relationship to Nature that is closer even than love. Perhaps it is only the artist who can really remember it.

Mystery pervades adult life also, however, as another story in *Miss Leonora*, "Two Pilgrims," amply demonstrates. In this straightforward and seemingly artless story, a seventeen-year-old boy tells of a trip he made from Memphis to a small town in northern Alabama as a chauffeur for his uncle, a cotton broker, and for his uncle's old friend, a lawyer. On the trip, the two older men discuss old times in the country they are passing through—"how good the bird hunting used to be" and the "fine people they knew who had once lived there." Their reminiscing is interrupted when in the old Natchez Trace section they spy a farmhouse on fire. Immediately, they order the boy to stop at the farmhouse and they rush in—with coats pulled over their heads "like a couple of hooded night riders"—to try to save the belongings in the house.

What is peculiar about the situation is the behavior of the farm couple who idly watch the rescue operations. The woman, alarmed at first that a bandit raid had been added to the horror of a burning house, later views with amused detachment the "bustle and bother" of her benefactors. "Well, they're right active," she admits, though she seems not to understand why they should take chances over the "junk" in the burning house. She herself is disinterested: "We heired this place from my grandma when she passed on last spring; the junk was all hern." Not until the lawyer runs out with a child's chamber pot is she reminded that her child might be inside the house. After frantic efforts to find the child, the rescuers finally discover it was with the father in the barn. The father, who seems just as unaware as the mother that "their house and most of their possessions were at that moment going up in flames," only mutters imprecations against the woman for sending the strangers vainly into the fire after the child.

The boy telling the story is appalled by the couple's incomprehensible reaction: "Surely there was some mystery, I said to myself, some questions that ought to be answered or asked." The mystery is accentuated by the imagery of the story, which suggests a descent into the nether world. The burning house, for instance, is in a clearing filled with smoldering, smoking stumps, creating an "infernal effect" over the whole scene. "One felt that the entire area within the dark ring of pinewoods might at any moment burst into flame," the boy narrator observes. In addition, the woman is described as looking like a "death's-head" and the two Good Samaritans as hooded like the pilgrims alluded to in the title.

If the infernal setting is a new experience for the narrator, it is only commonplace to the two older "pilgrims": "It was as if such a fire were an everyday occurrence in their lives and as if they lived always among such queer people as that afflicted poor-white farmer and his simple wife." The uncle and his friend refuse to accept the narrator's characterization of the place as "godforsaken" or even as "ugly." "Every countryside has its own kind of beauty," the uncle says. "It's up to you to learn to see it, that's all." The lawyer friend adds: "And if you don't see it, it's just your loss. Because it's *there.*" The only help they offer is the advice that "you would have to have seen that country thirty years ago to understand why it looks the way it does now."

Some things, then, Taylor seems to say, we are born accepting as natural and only with maturity come to recognize as mysterious, as "A Strange Story" points out. Other things we first take to be mysterious only to accept them as natural as age increases our experiences and, presumably, our wisdom, as "Two Pilgrims" indicates.

IV *"Born to Represent Something"*

"Miss Leonora When Last Seen," the title story of Taylor's 1963 volume, explores the mystery underlying an individual's life.

Because the individual being considered, Miss Leonora Logan, is an eccentric whose differences are noted by all about her, the problem of understanding human motivation is made unusually graphic. Miss Leonora is "quite an old lady," a retired school teacher, and "the last of the Logan family in Thomasville, a family that for a hundred years and more did all it could to impede the growth and progress" of the town. Because the county court has just condemned her inherited property to provide a site for the county's new consolidated high school, Miss Leonora has taken off in her 1942 Dodge convertible for parts unkown. Though she has taken such trips before, the indications are that this time she may not be coming back. Her cryptic postcards back to her old pupils in the town suggest only that she is circling through the surrounding states, "orbiting her native state of Tennessee."

The narrator, who was the first of Miss Leonora's "favorites" among her old students, fills in the background about her life and her personality, as much as this can be done: "Miss Leonora is an intellectual woman, and at the same time she is an extremely practical and simple kind of person. This makes it hard for any two people to agree on what she is really like. It is hard even for those of us who were her favorites when we went to school to her. For, in the end, we didn't really know her any better than anybody else did" (253). The narrator still recalls his first sight —almost a blinding vision—of Miss Leonora, when, at the age of five, he feverishly watched Miss Leonora, all dressed in white and with a "burning beauty" in her countenance, step ashore from a picnicker's rowboat as if she had "risen out of the water itself." The vision pierced his soul, he says, and awoke him to a beauty he had not dreamed of.

Other pictures supplement this early vision of her—sharp images of Miss Leonora standing out in a crowd at a drowning and at a fire at the old Thomasville Female Institute, of Miss Leonora entertaining her favorite students with coffee and cookies and conversation about "*Silas Marner* or Tom Paine or Cicero," of Miss Leonora off on one of her trips in either "a lot of outmoded finery" or in her dungarees and big poke bonnet. Always, Miss Leonora is the individualist who has her own ideas about what is good for Thomasville and for her favorites. For Thomasville, she agrees with the notion of her ancestors in the

Logan family that everything should be kept out which might possibly spoil the sweet dream of the town—things like a railroad, a county courthouse, a snuff factory or a cotton mill, a veterans' hospital, or a Civilian Conservation Corps camp. For those few students she has favored over the years, she urges a college education and entry into one of the professions in order "to populate the town with the sort of people she thought it ought to have." Her "mission" is the instruction of the town in her own values. "Looking back on those high-school days," the narrator says, "I know that all along she was watching me and others like me for some kind of sign from us—any sign—that would make us seem worthy of knowing what we wanted to know about her."

Even Miss Leonora's favorites never really give her this sign. Only one goes to college, and he comes back a pharmacist, not a physician; the narrator himself is nothing more than a hotel operator. And it is only in retrospect that these ex-students even understand what it was they wanted to know: "that the old lady had suffered for being just what she was—for being born with her cold, rigid, intellectual nature, and for being born to represent something that had never taken root in Thomasville and that would surely die with her." The pathos of her chosen role becomes clear only after the narrator breaks the news to her about the county's dispossessing of her and after she takes off on her last journey.

The terrible shock of the story is that Miss Leonora "when last seen" is no longer the eccentric individualist she has always been before. Instead of setting off in her fox-fur piece, diamond earrings, velvet hat, and lace choker, or in her other traveling costume of home-knit cardigan and dungarees, Miss Leonora has transformed herself into an ordinary person. The narrator is baffled: "For a minute I couldn't remember where it was I had seen this very woman before. Then it came to me. All that was lacking was a pair of pixie glasses with rhinestone rims, and a half dozen bracelets on her wrists. She was one of those old women who come out here from Memphis looking for antiques and country hams and who tell you how delighted they are to find a southern town that is truly unchanged" (274-75).

Miss Leonora has changed in more than appearance; she begins to say things that are "nothing like the things the real Miss Leonora used to say," but which are things "anybody might have said." One of these things is her admission that she was "unrealistic," that she had tried to be to the Thomasville children what she thought they "needed to have somebody be." "That's a mistake, always," she says. "One has to try to be with people what they want one to be." To the narrator, it is a little sad, then, to think of Miss Leonora alone in her old Dodge after her "change of heart," "wishing that either she had played the role of the spinster great lady the way it is usually played or that she had married some dirt farmer and spent her life working alongside him in the fields." With her role abandoned, there is no use even looking for her. "She will look too much like a thousand others," the narrator says; "and no doubt she will be driving on the highway the way everybody else does, letting other people pass her, dimming her lights for everyone."

Maybe the narrator is right when he says that "times do change, and the interests of one individual cannot be allowed to hinder the progress of a whole community." And maybe he is also right when he argues that Miss Leonora's periodic auto trips have been "escapes into a reality that is scattered in bits and pieces along the highways and back roads of the country she travels." But Peter Taylor seems to suggest between the lines that the community pays a high price for progress when it suffers the loss of the last remaining witness to the "traditions and institutions" that have been corrupted or lost in the life of the community. Mystery though it may be, that witness' life has a meaning that nothing else can ever duplicate.

V *"Beyond All the Good Sense and Reasonableness"*

Still more engrossing than the mystery of another's life and personality is the mystery of self. This mystery is illuminated in what is certainly the finest story in *Miss Leonora* and what is close to being the finest story Peter Taylor has ever written, "At the Drugstore."

It is almost as if Peter Taylor had determined to include the best elements of all his past stories in one masterpiece: the moral introspection of "Rain in the Heart" and "Two Ladies in Retirement," the mood creation of "*Je Suis Perdu*," the sharply etched characterizations of "A Long Fourth" and "Heads of Houses," the social consciousness of time and change of "The Scoutmaster" and "The Dark Walk," the simplicity of structure and complexity of theme of "1939" and "What You Hear From 'Em?" On the other hand, "At the Drugstore" has an individuality and originality that makes all its ingredients also seem fresh and new.

The hero of "At the Drugstore" is Matt Donelson, a man of thirty-five "back home on a visit," a semi-autobiographical character closely related in temperament and outlook to a number of other Taylor protagonists. The story recounts only one basic episode—the early morning visit Matt pays to the neighborhood drug-store where, as a teenager, he used to wait with his schoolmates for the special streetcar to the Country Day School. Ostensibly, Matt has returned to this haunt of his youth only to buy a bottle of shaving lotion, but unconsciously he is searching for an image of himself in the surroundings of his earlier, formative years.

The significance of the home visit is ironically foreshadowed in a brief exchange early in the story between Matt and his parents' new cook:

> "I suppose it feels good to you to be back home," she had said.
> "There's nothing like it," Matt had replied. "Absolutely nothing." (51)

The conversational cliché states a truth that Matt becomes more conscious of as the story progresses. Rising as he did at daybreak, while his parents, his wife, and his two boys are still sleeping, and seeing again the familiar cityscape about him, he feels his presence is "unreal," dreamlike, somehow dismaying. He recalls his arrival at the Union Depot the night before, where the remodeling of the depot lobby caused him momentarily to think himself in the wrong city.

The drugstore is also changed—except for the familiar pattern of the tile floor and the presence of the same old druggist of years past. In the artificial indigo tint of the fluorescent lights and in the early morning silence, Matt feels the drugstore has the "timeless quality" of a bank vault or a "small, out-of-the-way museum where the curator doesn't really expect or welcome visitors." When Matt sees not only the familiar face of Mr. Conway, the druggist, but, in the mirror behind Mr. Conway, "another familiar face (oh, *too familiar*)," he self-defensively puts on "the most impersonal, hard, out-of-town voice" he can muster. Later, the face in the mirror seems not the guilty school-boy face from the past it had at first seemed, but the face of an intruder, a "third, unfamiliar person on the scene, a person who, so to speak, ought still to have been asleep beside his wife back there in the family's guest room." This face, moreover, has expressed in its look, without his consciously putting it there, the same "impersonal, hard, out-of-town" quality he had consciously put in his voice.

Memories sweep over Matt Donelson as he finds excuses to linger in the store. He recalls, particularly, the harassments (mischievous and sometimes even obscene) which the Country Day school boys had once piled on Mr. Conway, but which Matt himself had never taken part in. So well does he remember the old image of Mr. Conway as an authority-figure, that he finds himself at one point "momentarily insane" with repressed rage and ready to assault "the old Scrooge, the old bastard." The scrap between the two is avoided, but Matt knows that he will never be able to explain to anyone how near he came to unprecedented violence. "How unlike him it would have been, what an anomaly, how incongruous with everything else in a life that was going so well."

As he returns home for breakfast with his parents, his wife, and his children, he alternates between feelings of elation and feelings of despair and "of some other emotion less easily or less willingly identified . . . like regret for lost opportunities." The barrier he still feels between himself and his family can only be explained by a "kind of nonsense":

> It seemed to him now that he had gone to that drugstore on purpose this morning, that he had planned the whole adventure before he ever left New York. It had been intended to satisfy some passing and unnamed need of his, but the adventure had cut too deep into his memory and into what was far more than mere memory. Inadvertently he had penetrated beyond all the good sense and reasonableness that made life seem worthwhile—or even tolerable. And through the breach, beyond, behind or beneath all this, he was now confronted by a thing that had a face and a will of its own. It was there threatening not only him and his father but the others too. Its threat was always present really, in him and in every man. It was in women too, no doubt, but they were so constituted that they never lost sight of it, were always on their guard, were dealing with it every moment of their lives. (78)

This nameless "Thing" he finally recognizes, catching a glimpse of his own reflection in the glass of a dark still-life painting (dead fish and dead, dull pheasants) above the family sideboard; the reflection appears to him "as the very face of that Thing he had uncovered," a "monstrous obtrusion on the relatively bright scene that was reflected all around it—the innocent scene at the breakfast table behind Matt." Observing the happy chattering family, he thinks: "How dearly he loved them all! And how bitterly the Thing showing its face in the glass hated them!"

Though Matt himself soon laughingly dismisses the "nonsense" about the "boogy man in the glass," the reader cannot so easily forget it. And when Matt, reconciled and united in a new understanding with his father and his family, dramatically peels his breakfast orange without a single break on the "thin inner pellicle" and lifts up the fruit "unscathed and whole" for all to see, the reader senses he has watched the excision and contemplation of something far more significant than an ordinary orange. He has, symbolically, seen the secret soul of a moral man.

VI *The Uncollected Stories*

At the time he compiled the *Miss Leonora* collection in 1963, Peter Taylor left a half-dozen of his stories—mostly early efforts—uncollected. Since he usually includes in a new volume just the work published since the immediately preceding collection,[8] it was not surprising that he passed over these same stories when compiling *Collected Stories* in 1969. Though now doomed to oblivion, all six are valuable in defining Taylor's talent.

The first two of these stories appeared in the March and April issues of the short-lived Mississippi magazine *River* in 1937 and were probably written while Taylor was a freshman at Southwestern College at Memphis.[9] Appropriately for a fictional debut, the first story published was entitled "The Party."[10] The second had a title indicative of the pseudosophistication which characterized it: "The Lady Is Civilized."[11]

"The Party" introduced the subject that was to become Peter Taylor's own special property: the migration of rural Southerners to the big cities. In this initial venture, however, the central character is not one who leaves forever, but one who comes back to till an inherited farm. He is Albert Winston, who gives the party at his farm as a reunion for his old friends who have permanently replaced rural life with urban life. The secret motivation for the party is Albert's compulsion to test his young wife's devotion to their country way of life. He is afraid that he will find out "that she had married him only because the other boys had gone away and met city girls and forgotten her" and that she will want him "to let her go." She, however, has only had her contentment with pastoral delights restored by her contact with the city-dwellers.

The sociological orientation of "The Party" seems to be that of the Nashville Agrarians. "I remember," one of the older characters says, "when the parents or grandparents of every one of the boys that will be here to-night lived on a farm and in a house very much like the house Albert Winston lives in now." Even Albert's family "left the country same as everybody else did many years ago"; but Albert, who was already thought queer for reading books, quit college after two years and took over the farm of a ne'er-do-well uncle, after which "the whole town turned against him." Detail after detail in the story builds up the picture of Albert's life as leisurely, cultured, and full of sincere fellowship. The vision, in short, is of the ideal enunciated by John Crowe Ransom, Allen Tate, and the other Vanderbilt Agrarians in *I'll Take My Stand.* It is a borrowed vision which does not appear, as we have noted, in the mature work of Peter Taylor without heavy ironic qualification.

The second *River* story, "The Lady Is Civilized," is of interest primarily because it contains as part of its melodramatic plot the incident of a Negro crime—the murder and dismemberment of a Negro man by his wife and her lover—which was to crop up twenty-two years later as part of "A Friend and Protector." This incident is about the only connection this story has with Taylor's later work, for it is obviously the self-conscious effort of an immature writer striving for effect. The soap-opera subject (an ambitious wife selling herself to a wealthy old roué), the belabored symbols (a picture of Judas to suggest the wife's betrayal, for instance), the affected prose style ("The rain was beating murderously down . . ." begins all three sentences in the first paragraph)—all these are features far removed from what Taylor was doing just a couple of years later.

Another early story much inferior to the later work is "The School Girl," published in 1942 in another little magazine,[12] about a young girl reminiscent of Rhoda in William March's *The Bad*

Seed. "She's never been anything but a joy to us," one of the characters says about Jane Ellen, who has just brought home a perfect report card. But Taylor gives away his whole story when he describes "the single curl which was brushed down precisely in the center of the girl's forehead." Though, when she's good, she's very very good, we know at once that, when she's bad, she's going to be horrid. Fortunately, being horrid in this story only means impaling a live butterfly for a bonnet decoration, which hardly qualifies Jane Ellen as another Temple Drake or Regina Hubbard.

"Attendant Evils," a story included in a 1944 Vanderbilt anthology,[13] comes closer to being good Peter Taylor material. Written as a letter from a Southern matron to her married daughter, it treats one of his favorite subjects; the tactics of running a southern household. In this instance, the setting is wartime, and the matron recounts her trouble in locating a Negro nursemaid to help the daughter. The impudence and unreliability of the available servant help is to the matron one of the "attendant evils" of the war. But the between-the-lines irony of the author makes it evident that the supercilious condescension and domineering patricianism of the matron is one of the attendant evils of a long-lasting war between classes and races in the South. The best part of the story is the humor inherent in the passive defiance through which the "stupid, sullen" Negroes frustrate the irate white woman. The point, however, seems to stem from the social criticism underlying the comic situations.

The remaining two stories not included in the 1963 collection are probably good enough to be preserved. "Uncles," a 1949 publication,[14] presents a Kenyon College freshman returning to St. Louis for Christmas vacation. "Nerves," which first appeared in 1961,[15] develops a story within a story, as the narrator listens to the anecdotes of a stranger he meets on a Nashville park bench. The family the Kenyon freshman returns to in "Uncles" is one of those large Taylor families where collateral relationships are nearly as important as lineal ones. Visiting with his uncles and great-uncles, the freshman begins to feel that their "one-dimensional, exclusively masculine view of life" represents not a change from, but a continuation of, the dormitory life he has known at the all-male college. When he finally does contact again his mother and female relatives, he realizes that he will never again be able to talk to them "except in the specific role of a man."

This realization is regrettable to him as an embryonic artist, because he knows that the bourgeois mentality of his father and uncles rules out the artistic life for men: "It suddenly became clear that everything clever, gentle, and light belonged to women and the world they lived in. To men belonged only the more serious things in life, the deadly practical things—constructive ideas, profitable jobs, stories with morals, jokes with points." There is little the young man can do but try to "adjust" and "assimilate" the things that are to be his.

In "Nerves," also a story about adjustment to the lot which cultural circumstances impose on the individual, the narrator is a Nashville native back home on a visit. While watching his little son play in Centennial Park, he converses with another father, a man of his own generation, about the nervous solicitude each has been showing for the playing children. Soon the second man has launched into a "totally unexpected" and "quite remarkable" speech about changes that have taken place in the city since his childhood. Symbolizing the stages of change are the various means of public transportation used in different eras: the mule cars of his grandfather's day, the streetcars he himself remembers so well from his youth, and the buses of the present period. Each epoch is captured in little vignettes illustrative of the prevailing social attitudes.

Contemporary mores seem to be summed up by an incident the man relates that occurred recently on one of the "big, smelly buses" which "sneak along through traffic with no bells to clang, no rights of their own, no dignity of any kind." It is a shocking incident—"like a wirephoto from some scene of trouble on the other side of the world"—in which the man and the bus driver had to stand helplessly by while two white hoodlums menaced a Negro girl in the rear seat. Though the Negro girl's knife successfully held the youths at bay, the experience makes the man who observed it "uneasy" in a general way about the kind of life in which a police siren is a "comforting" and "familiar" sound. So graphic is the second man's story, and so sympathetic are his ideas and attitudes to that of the first man, that the original narrator confesses that he gave "silent prompting and encouragement" to what was actually a vicarious articulation of his own thoughts.

Despite the long monologue which makes up the bulk of the

story, "Nerves" is a convincing piece of fiction developed with considerable craftsmanship, especially in the way in which it creates the illusion of impromptu speech. If there is anything which "Nerves," "Uncles," and the other uncollected pieces have in common, it may be only that each makes its point a little more obviously than the usual Taylor story does. In these six uncollected stories, it is fairly easy to extract a central theme and to say where the author's sympathies lie. Most of these stories move close either to satire, on the one hand, or to romantic excess, on the other; in short, these stories either do, or tend to do, two things which Peter Taylor's best fiction never does—to oversimplify the subject and to underestimate the reader.

VII *Collected Stories*

For a second retrospective collection with a new publisher[16] in 1969, Taylor revived two stories from *A Long Fourth* and four from *The Widows of Thornton* (all of which had also been included in *Miss Leonora*), six from *Happy Families*, and four of the new stories from *Miss Leonora*.

Collected Stories also contains five new tales, all remindful of techniques and motifs in earlier works. The theme of betrayal, present to some degree in nearly all the older stories, comes to the fore because of the emphasis it gets in the two fine new stories opening the volume, "Dean of Men" and "First Heat." The first, another leisurely three-generation memoir story, represents a college administrator telling his student son how the boy's great-grandfather, grandfather, and father had all suffered different kinds of betrayal and how each had had to seek afterwards a way to "somehow go on living among men"; " it is a strange world," he says, "in which an old man must tell a young man this." "First Heat," a short straightforward dramatic story, treats betrayal from the point of view of the betrayer: a state senator must face his conscience in the person of his wife after he has withdrawn his promised support from a colleague on a crucial vote. Though neither story breaks much new ground in matter or form, both are superb examples of the usual Taylor craftsmanship.

Two other works are only mildly impressive, weakly echoing themes from *The Widows of Thornton.* "Mrs. Billingsby's Wine," a story about a young Memphis housewife calling on a grande dame from her old home town, is rather artificially told in the historical present in the manner of the very early story, "Allegiance." The young woman, Shirley Barnes, expects to be snubbed by the dowager, Mrs. Billingsby, but hopes eventually to win her patronage for her own social climbing. Surprisingly, Mrs. Billingsby is gracious and friendly and happily reminisces with Shirley over their mutual hometown of Blackwell, Tennessee. Listening to her, however, Shirley realizes that, though they were once next-door neighbors, their differences in social status, age, and attitude toward urban progress leave them no common ground; even their memories of Blackwell seem to be of two separate towns.

"The Elect," Taylor's first story since "The Dark Walk" to be published in one of the slick women's magazines,[17] describes the emotions of the domestically inclined wife of a gubernatorial candidate the day after her husband wins the election. Her relief that the campaign ordeal of living like "show people" is over turns to an unnamed anxiety as she waits her husband's thanks for her campaign assistance; the anxiety turns first to tears and then to stoic resignation when she finally realizes her husband wants her to continue the public role she hates. Never again will she have the old domestic pleasures of paying her own household bills, of hemming her own skirts, of knowing the arrangement of her own kitchen. Like the biblical Ruth, whom she had once cited on a campaign platform, she must follow her husband whither he goes and his show people must now be her people, for she is one of those "elect" who are chosen from the many called to take on uncongenial duties in an ever-changing world.

Much more complex in both form and content is a highly-acclaimed *Kenyon Review* story, "There."[18] As in the story "Nerves," a first-person narrator meets a stranger from his hometown (a nameless "inland city") and finds himself listening to a long monologue full of subjective reminiscing. If the emphasis in "Nerves" was on the differences between eras, the emphasis in "There" is on the differences between places—specifically between *"There"* (the hometown) and the rest of the world. The narrator and his new acquaintance, who meet aboard a ship, are united by their common point of origin and by their common estrangement from that origin. But the middle-aged narrator also feels that the elderly Mr. Charles Varnell is "the kind of shipboard acquaintance you make who never seems real afterward" and that the thirty or forty years that separate them in age make them "strangers to one another" as "no distance across the surface of the earth nowadays, and no difference in nationality," could possibly do. The old man, though reticent about himself, is "voluble enough on other subjects—particularly on the subject of *other* people." And it is memories of the people back *there* that touch him off.

In that city were the Busbys, the old man recalls, who never washed. And the Jenkinses who all got extremely fat. "It used to seem to me that every family there had some awful deficiency—I might almost say affliction—that marked them as a family," Mr. Varnell says. "The astonishing thing to me was always that the Busbys, like the Jenkinses and other families with equally marked peculiarities, remained in the very cream of society *there*. Nobody there minded them as they were, and so why need they change themselves?" The one family he had found "interesting and admirable" was the Morris family, each member of which was distinguished for individuality and apparent lack of family traits. When he was a young man studying for a diplomatic career, Mr. Varnell fell in love with pretty Laura Nell, the practical joker of the Morris family, who chided Varnell for his inability to forgive people their faults. Laura Nell made a bargain then with Varnell: if he could guess the secret terrible trait the individualistic Morrises all had in common, then she would forgive him everything. Varnell eventually found out from Laura Nell's mother that the girl was alluding to a grim little joke of her grandfather's: "He used to say that the Morrises were all alike in at least one respect: they all had to die some time or other." Laura Nell's last practical joke was to prove the grandfather right—by contracting an inexplicable fatal disease and dying.

Varnell is, then, a kind of modern cross between Melville's Taji in *Mardi* and Hawthorne's Aylmer in "The Birthmark." Like Taji, he is contemptuous of the flawed human beings about him and searches for a phantom ideal in the person of an elusive maiden. Like Aylmer, he discovers mortality, the family flaw or birthmark that all men, even those closest to the ideal, must share. But Varnell's story is not the transparent allegory which the comparison might suggest. Between Hawthorne-Melville and Peter Taylor intervened Henry James, and the Jamesian method makes all the difference. Peter Taylor has not presented Varnell's story directly but has placed it in a narrative frame of the sort James used with *The Turn of the Screw.* Varnell himself is a half-century removed from his own experience; he is, we are told, "like a man delving into a trunk he had packed away years ago and who did not know, himself, what he would come upon next." And the first narrator, who as we have already seen, considers himself an inevitable stranger to Varnell, refracts the meaning as the story passes through his mediating consciousness. Every literal detail therefore undergoes at least three stages of ironic qualification: Varnell's mature sophistication enables him to recognize certain foolishness in his early point of view; the first narrator's academic detachment permits him to detect blind spots even in Varnell's present vision; and, between the lines, Peter Taylor's own auctorial presence suggests the limitations of the first narrator's insight.

Unfortunately, limited space and the publisher's understandable desire for variety kept several of Taylor's best recent pieces out of *Collected Stories.* Despite an overall familiarity in subject and style, all offer a few surprising new insights, as admirably demonstrated by the 1964 story, "Throughway."[19] As a story of the contradictory reactions of an old couple when their house is condemned to make way for highway construction, "The Throughway" is remarkable for its avoidance of the expected sentimental clichés. Compared to this story, in fact, "Miss Leonora When Last Seen," which concerned a similar dispossession by the right of eminent domain, might appear quite conventional and almost maudlin. In "The Throughway," Taylor goes to great pains to strip his situation of those possibilities which might give it undue social significance. Unlike Miss Leonora, Harry and Irene are nobodies; and they do not in any ostensible way represent any tradition or any historic values. Even the house they are losing is rented, not inherited or even earned by work and sacrifice. The house is, moreover, not a thing of beauty, of economic worth, or of sentimental attachment. The story obviously, then, cannot be the expected melodrama about old values being crowded out by new.

The conflict in "The Throughway," in fact, is not even between the old couple and the forces of progress, but within the couple, between the husband and the wife. For it is only Harry who opposes the throughway; Irene readily accepts the inevitable. As a result, they are not found as "two who [are] allied against an intruding world" but unexpectedly as "two adversaries." What Taylor focuses on in the story is the motivation which inspires the opposite reactions, the interior evaluation which each gives to the fact of dispossession. Here, again, none of the predictable explanations will unravel the mystery of why the woman cares so little about her home, or why the man cares so much. Harry and Irene themselves do not at the beginning of the story understand their own inner reasons; and, when some understanding comes at the end, the understanding doesn't help.

By presenting the situation alternately through the consciousnesses of the two old people, Taylor commits himself to no single, simple explanation. "I own nothing," Harry says at one point. "I made up my mind early in life to ask for nothing. I thought that nothing was something they could never take away from me." But at another point, Irene insists: "Harry, my darling, all along you've wanted *everything*, which is what everybody wants—not nothing. But something inside you made you feel that it was wrong." All that can be safely said is that the issue is one of success and failure as related to ownership. But it is through that issue that "the world" comes in and estranges human being from human being, even husband from wife. And that mysterious estrangement is the fate to which Harry and Irene must turn, at the story's end, in "awful resignation."

Two other recent stories," The End of Play"[20] and "A Cheerful Disposition,"[21] reveal how enduring Taylor's fictional interests are. The elements are all so familiar, in fact, that the reader only gradually becomes convinced that they do add up to something new. In "The End of Play," for instance, the locale once again is St. Louis in the 1930's. The characters are a well-to-do Southern family transplanted from their hometown of Thornton, Tennessee, the same country town which had such an influence on the characters of *The Widows of Thornton.* The form is the autobiographical memoir form used so effectively in *Happy Families Are All Alike*. The conflicts include those between the young and the old, the traditional and the new, the South and the Midwest —conflicts that motivated the drama in *Tennessee Day in St. Louis.* And, finally, there is the young protagonist revealed "during those years of life when one is taking his measure of the world."

The title "The End of Play" has a double significance. It refers literally to the conclusion of "the Convention game" which the narrator was playing all that Presidential campaign summer of 1932, a game the narrator (then eleven years old) made up himself in imitation of the nominating conventions he had listened to on the radio. It refers also to the end of the childish "fantasies and play-pretends" which up to that time the boy had been wont to engage in.

Both types of play have expressed the boy's conflict with his father that summer. The father, it seems, has wanted his son to accompany him back to Thornton on the frequent trips he has been making while trying to decide whether he should "hole up in that little Southern town" until the end of the Depression. But the father has not wanted the boy along "just for the ride"; he has wanted the boy to say first that he wants to know his relatives and to be acquainted with the town and the country his family came from. And this admission, the boy in his own pride has not been able to make. As a result, the father has resented the activity which the boy does engage in, and the boy has put into his game the hidden tensions and anxieties that he feels about his relationship to his father and to his familial background. As a native St. Louisian, the boy has ambivalent feelings about his ancestral home and the possibly imminent move there.

As part of the Convention game, the boy invents a delegate from Tennessee—"a sort of Senator Claghorn created ten years or so before the radio reproduced him"—who employs all the florid and chauvinistic rhetoric the boy has picked up from speeches of his Southern forebears. (Some of the jingoistic phrases the boy uses in impersonating this burlesque politician are, incidentally, identical with those Taylor gives to Senator Caswell in *Tennessee Day in St. Louis.*) The boy is both fascinated and repelled by his own creation, for he represents the mixed emotions the boy has toward Thornton. To what extent the boy uses the imaginary convention delegate as a persona through which he can attempt communication—both belligerent and conciliatory—with his father, he himself cannot say. But at the end of the Convention game, the father-son antagonism has expended itself, and the boy gladly acquiesces in the father's decision to move the family back to Tennessee.

A different kind of playing is depicted in "A Cheerful Disposition," in which the games are the rituals surrounding death. The protagonist, Frank Lacy, is a middle-aged New Yorker who returns to his hometown for the funeral of his eldest brother, the first family member of his generation to die. Frank, who prides himself on his "cheerful disposition," at first is pleased by the naturalness and familiarity of the attendant rituals—"very much like the old days"; he thinks his hometown "a splendid town to be coming home to" with its "provincial stylishness" and a kind of "fairy-tale perfection about it." He has "a childlike illusion of relating to all about him," until he ironically mistakes an undertaker for a member of the family and then conversely his own brother for an undertaker!

The "joy and transport" of "his pilgrimage home" are shattered, however, by his sister Norma, who descends on him like "a strange, new spirit" for "the sole purpose of contradicting all his own impressions of the past two days." After Norma hysterically denounces various members of the family and depicts all the funeral events as "dismally depressing" and "miserably grotesque," both Frank and his wife Janet are left stunned and incredulous. Janet, who has seemed a paragon of efficiency and detachment, explains Norma's outburst as the sign of her fear of death; then Janet suddenly becomes hysterical herself.

Frank, realizing his practical Janet is "no less afraid than the others," wonders why he is not hysterical, too. "Was his cheerful disposition really only shallowness?" he asks himself. He finally concludes that he merely has a different awareness of where life lies: for him, it is to be found in the carefree irresponsibility of the nightspots of his adolescence, in "freedom from the confines the other members of his family knew." But, as he falls asleep soon after, he has a terrifying dream in which he sees himself in his brother's coffin. This dream, "born of being home," convinces him that home can mean "a glimpse of childhood" no longer; home is now forevermore a confrontation with mortality, the ultimate devastation wrought by the changes of time.

Between Taylor's earliest stories and his latest, then, there has not been any great disparity in subject matter or in theme. Nor has there been any revolutionary shift in artistic method; structure, mood, tone, style, point of view have all developed new potentialities without changing their basic patterns. As early as

"The Scoutmaster" and "A Long Fourth," Peter Taylor had already found an appropriate form for his individual vision. If recent stories like "A Cheerful Disposition" or "The End of Play" offer something new, it is principally a broadening at the peripheries of a vision that has long seen deep into the mysteries of the human soul.

CHAPTER 8

The Achievement of Peter Taylor

I *The Vision of a Southerner*

PETER TAYLOR is first and foremost a Southern writer. Any assessment of his achievement which ignored the living relationship between the author and his region would be incomplete. Yet any assessment which merely dismissed Peter Taylor as a member of that amorphous something known as the "Southern School" would be not only incomplete but seriously misleading. The South which Peter Taylor writes about is hardly recognizable as the one which inspired the earlier generation of writers in the Southern Literary Renaissance. As Louis D. Rubin, Jr., has pointed out: "The South that Faulkner, Wolfe, Tate, Ransom, and their contemporaries knew when they were growing up in the years before the First World War was vastly different from the South between the wars. Thus the present generation of Southern writers, most of whom were born in the 1920's and grew to manhood in the 1930's and 1940's, many of them serving in the armed forces during the Second World War, writes out of a different experience, and the fiction and the poetry show it."[1]

The difference, however, has more to do with the cultural vantage point from which the change in the South was experienced than it does with the birthdate of the writer. Thus, Carson McCullers, who was born the same year as Taylor, has a vision of the South closely kin to the Faulknerian. So, too, have Truman Capote and Flannery O'Connor, who were born seven and eight years after Taylor. On the other hand, some writers older than Taylor (Randall Jarrell) and some younger (William Styron) share a new vision which contrasts sharply with the old.

Some of the more noted attributes of the Faulknerians simply cannot be found in Peter Taylor. "Violence dominates Southern fiction written since 1930," Louise Gossett says with full justice in her study of the recent fiction of the region.[2] But violence is obviously not one of the staples in Taylor's writing. The only really violent event even alluded to in Taylor's stories is the murder and dismemberment of a Negro man by his wife and her lover, an incident recounted twice, once in the very early story "The Lady Is Civilized" and again in "A Friend and Protector." Though the anecdote must have had a powerful hold on Taylor's imagination, since he used it twice, in neither story does he fully dramatize it or exploit its sensational qualities; only in the first treatment, in fact, is it even central to the story. There are no rapes, castrations, lynchings, duels, barnburnings, or cannibalistic orgies anywhere in Taylor's fictional world. Though there is an attempted suicide in *Tennessee Day in St. Louis* and an accidental death in "An Overwhelming Question," the only major violence in Taylor's whole canon is the off-stage murderous rampage of Harry in *A Stand in the Mountains*, a play that is neither typical nor wholly successful.

Peter Taylor does not rely, either, on the use of the grotesque to present his vision of the modern South. Tennessee Williams has explained that Southern authors write about "dreadful things" because, if they do not wish to write lengthy interior monologues in the style of Joyce and Proust, compression and distortion of experience into grotesque symbols is the only method left by which they can effectively express their sense of the awfulness in contemporary life.[3] Peter Taylor does not lack this sense of the awfulness of life, but he has found an alternative way of presenting it. His method is close to Chekhov's: he shows us sensitive characters discovering the dreadful in the trivia of their daily lives. Helen Ruth Lovell in "A Wife of Nashville" and Matt Donelson in "At the Drugstore" come as close to existential anguish as the more dramatic characters of a Tennessee Williams or a Carson McCullers. In the rare stories where Taylor attempts to compress the dreadful into grotesque symbols (as in "A Spinster's Tale" and "Venus, Cupid, Folly and Time"), he gravely endangers the psychological verisimilitude which is the hallmark of his most distinguished work.

Just as Taylor almost always eschews the gothic distortion which turns action into violence and character into the grotesque, so too he avoids other types of exaggeration prevalent in much Southern literature. He does not, for instance, indulge in the fancy flights of rhetoric which make many Southern writers sound like Jefferson Davis Day orators; his style is cool, classically simple, urbane. Nor does he partake of the raw, earthy, frontier-type humor which dominates works like Faulkner's *The Hamlet* and Eudora Welty's *The Robber Bridegroom* and which delightfully flavors the work of most contemporary Southerners. Though his grandfather and great-uncle, Governor Bob and Governor Alf Taylor, were both practictioners of this tall-tale comedy, Taylor himself writes about people far removed from the folksy background of bucolic manners which made that type of humor possible. William Peden, in his study of the American short story, has classified Taylor among the "Jane Austens of Metropolis and Suburbia," a category that aptly suggests Taylor's discreetly ironic brand of humor.[4] Taylor also differs from many other Southern writers in that he does not try to enlarge his stories to epic proportions and therefore has no need to rely on a substructure of mythic parallels to carry the extra symbolic weight.

Despite these departures from some of the standard features of the so-called Southern school, Peter Taylor does in many ways reveal his kinship to his fellow writers in the Southern Renaissance. He has, first of all, that all-important sense of "place" which seems to color the whole sensibility of a Southerner. "Place can focus the gigantic, voracious eye of genius, and bring its gaze to point," Eudora Welty has said.[5] Taylor's eye is indeed focused by place, but it is not focused on quite the expected point. Whereas the usual Southern writer zooms in on either the anachronistic plantation home or the fading small country town, Taylor altogether avoids the first and only sparingly uses the second.

The country town does have great symbolic value in his narratives, as part of the remembered background of his characters; but it is only occasionally the actual setting for a story. Peter Taylor knows Southern culture in this prototypic form, but he also knows it (far better than many of his fellow Southern writers do) in two of its most important modern manifestations: the progressive urban center of the "New South" (Nashville, Memphis), and the expatriate community pocketed in a Northern or Midwestern metropolis (St. Louis, Chicago, Detroit). His stories concentrate on the relatively unexplored manners and mores of these two urban groups, especially as they relate back to the country town which anteceded them. As a result, his fiction has a subject and a setting virtually untouched in the rest of contemporary literature.

Taylor also shares the typical Southern preoccupation with history, tradition, and change. Even here, however, Taylor's attitude toward the subject represents a significant shift: his tone is not so much nostalgic as it is ironic. When he creates characters who yearn for a return to past values (Uncle Jake in "The Scoutmaster" or Miss Patty Bean in "Their Losses"), he presents the characters and their opinions objectively from an external point of view; even if the tone of the story as a whole is sympathetic to the character's ideas, there are always little contrasts to provide ironic qualification. Thus, he may not make fun of Miss Leonora in "Miss Leonora When Last Seen" or of Aunt Munsie in "What You Hear From 'Em?" to the point of satire, but he does direct the reader's attention to details which prevent him from accepting wholeheartedly the philosophic position of the character.

Finally, it may be said that Peter Taylor's affinity to the Southern Renaissance is found in his allegiance to certain institutional values largely disregarded in contemporary life. Robert Penn Warren was the first to suggest that Taylor's real subject was "the disintegration of families . . . the attrition of old loyalties, the breakdown of old patterns, and the collapse of old values"; and Andrew Lytle and Ashley Brown have been among those echoing this interpretation.[6] Certainly it is true, as Warren states, that Taylor treats an urban world "vastly uncertain of itself and the ground of its values, caught in a tangle of modern commercialism and traditions and conventions gone to seed, confused among pieties and pretensions." Yet this is only one small part of Taylor's total revelation. Furthermore, the Faulknerian connotations of such a theme are almost totally lacking in Peter Taylor, who is not concerned to create a myth of modern degeneration or a saga of the sinking South. Taylor is not "sociological," even in the flattering sense in which Tolstoy or George Eliot might be said to be so; the family in his work is not treated as an institution but as one part of a complex background for personal discoveries and developments.

II *The Voice of a Gentleman*

"Paradox has characterized the development of the short story in America," William Peden, one of the foremost experts on the subject, has asserted. Peden's point is that, "Although it is the only major literary form of essentially American origin and the only one in which American writers have always tended to excel, it has for decades been considered a parvenu, and until very recently most critics have refused to consider it as important as the more traditional forms of poetry, drama, and the novel."[7] The paradox of Peter Taylor's literary reputation is a part of this more general paradox involving the short story as a genre.

Whatever recognition Peter Taylor deserves, he merits on the basis of his achievement in the short-story medium. His one novella, *A Woman of Means,* is too slight to build a reputation on, and his three plays have not yet been put to the test of professional production. He is reportedly working on a novel trilogy and a group of plays which may someday put him in the literary limelight.[8] In the meantime, he must be judged primarily on his accomplishments in short fiction.

Even here, in his favorite form, Peter Taylor's achievement is not that of an innovator. Taylor has compared himself to Trollope, and his position in the history of the twentieth-century American short story is indeed analogous to that of Trollope in the history of the nineteenth-century English novel. "There are two kinds of taste in the appreciation of imaginative literature: the taste for emotions of surprise, and the taste for emotions of recognition," Henry James noted in his essay on Trollope. "It is the latter that Trollope gratifies, and he gratifies it the more that the medium of his own mind, through which we see what he shows us, gives a confident direction to our sympathy."[9] Peter Taylor gratifies this same taste for emotions of recognition, and he gratifies it through much the same method which James attributes to Trollope—through his "complete appreciation of the usual." Another way of putting it would be to say that Taylor takes the commonplace subject matter of a William Dean Howells and runs it through the rarefied mind of a Henry James.

In neither technique nor theme is Taylor likely to seem startling or disturbing. Only in a few early stories does he try such self-conscious experimental techniques as dramatic monologue ("A Walled Garden"), montage structure ("Sky Line"), present-tense narration ("Allegiance"), and gothic setting and grotesque characterization ("A Spinster's Tale"). The techniques of his later stories are, generally speaking, far less contrived than these. Nowhere does Taylor employ the morbid subject matter, the disjunctive structure and style, the abstruse symbolism, or the scatalogical diction characteristic of many of his more famous contemporaries. He is never brutal, coarse, shocking; but neither is he precious, coy, titillating. The voice that speaks in his stories is essentially the voice of a gentleman—cultured but not dilettantish, ironic but not cynical, urbane but not foppish, sensitive but not sentimental. In short, Taylor preserves what was best in the genteel tradition in American letters without any of the mawkishness and prudery often associated with it.

Taylor's themes, like his techniques, neither exploit nor affront popular taste. There is little that is daring, iconoclastic, revolutionary in what Peter Taylor has to say. To note this characteristic, however, is not to say that he is banal or platitudinous. Limiting himself artistically to a narrow range of experience, Taylor nevertheless probes deeply within this circumscribed area, preferring generally to make a refinement on an old idea than to propose a totally new one. "And he has always been content to use his material; he never argues about it," Walter Sullivan has observed.[10] His own philosophic position seems one of mild, gentlemanly skepticism. Like Chekhov, he is more inclined to try to state questions correctly than to attempt definitive answers. He has, as Warren long ago pointed out, "a disenchanted mind, but a mind that nevertheless understands and values enchantment."[11] Thus, Taylor neither builds up new castles in the air from his own fancies, nor tears down those built by others. He has the rare gift of being able to criticize and appreciate simultaneously, to mix nostalgia and irony in a compound which retains the piquancy of both.

Peter Taylor's greatest achievement is probably his ability to create, within the restrictive confines of a short story, characters with a richness and complexity rarely found even in novels. "We care what happens to people only in proportion as we know what people are," James argued;[12] and Peter Taylor provides the proof for the dictum. Uncle Jake, Josie Carlson, Harriet Wilson, Sylvia Harrison, Aunt Munsie, Helen Ruth Lovell, the Tolliver family, Henry Parker, Matt Donelson, Franny and Miles Miller—these are the glory of Peter Taylor's art. "In the final analysis," William

Peden has aptly said, "Taylor's fiction is meaningful because his characters are meaningful."[13]

In an age when alienation seems man's inevitable lot, Peter Taylor offers a quiet hope and consolation. When we read his stories, we are gently reassured that man has not yet completely lost the capacity to know and, on occasion, to love.

Notes and References

Preface

1. For representative comments of reviewers, see *A Library of Literary Criticism,* ed. Dorothy Nyren (New York, 1960), pp. 480-82. For a selective listing of general criticism and reviews, see the Bibliography.

2. J. F. Powers, review of *A Long Fourth, Commonweal,* XLVIII (June 25, 1948), 262.

Chapter One

1. The basic biographical facts about Peter Taylor can be gleaned from Robert Penn Warren's Introduction to Taylor's *A Long Fourth and Other Stories* (New York, 1948), pp. vii-viii; Stanley J. Kunitz and Howard Haycraft, "Taylor, Peter," *Twentieth Century Authors: First Supplement* (New York, 1955), p. 986; and Joint Committee of the North Carolina English Teachers Association and the North Carolina Library Association, "Taylor, Peter," *North Carolina Authors: A Selective Handbook* (Chapel Hill, 1952), p. 120. Material in this chapter has also been compiled from scattered newspaper items, dust jacket sketches, notes on contributors in magazines, publisher's press releases, and documents in the Kenyon College archives and alumni files. In a letter to the author dated October 23, 1966, Peter Taylor graciously made corrections and additions to the assembled material.

2. "The End of Play," *Virginia Quarterly Review,* XLI (Spring, 1965), 264-65.

3. *Biographical Directory of the American Congress, 1774-1961* (Washington, D. C., 1961) contains biographical sketches on Alfred Alexander Taylor, p. 1691; Nathaniel Green Taylor, p. 1695; and Robert Love Taylor, pp. 1695-96. See also the *DAB,* Vol. XVIII, for material on Alfred Alexander Taylor, p. 313, and Robert Love Taylor, pp. 341-43; these *DAB* articles also have brief bibliographies. For data on Taylor's father, see "Taylor, Hillsman," in *Who's Who in the South and Southwest,* 1950, and *Who's Who in America,* 1962-63.

4. Such stories would include "Two Ladies in Retirement," "The Dark Walk," "The Other Times," "Promise of Rain," "The Little Cousins," "A Strange Story," "Uncles," and "The End of Play."

5. The following account is based on notes of Peter Taylor in a letter to the author, October 23, 1966.

6. "Biographical Notes," in *The House of Fiction,* ed. Caroline Gordon and Allen Tate (New York, 1950), p. 648.

7. Warren, Introduction to *A Long Fourth,* p. vii.

8. The basic principles of the Agrarian movement can be found in the book by Ransom and eleven other Southerners, *I'll Take My Stand* (New York, 1962), originally published in 1930. See Alexander Karanikas, *Tillers of a Myth* (Madison, 1966), for a good discussion of the Agrarian philosophy.

9. For typical comments, see "The Scoutmaster," "A Long Fourth," "Their Losses," "Miss Leonora When Last Seen," and "Nerves."

10. For a brief historical account of the New Criticism, see William Van O'Connor, *An Age of Criticism 1900-1950* (Chicago, 1952).

11. Both Mrs. Taylor and Taylor himself have written reminiscences of their friendship with Jarrell in *Randall Jarrell, 1914-1965,* ed. by Robert Lowell, Peter Taylor, and Robert Penn Warren (New York, 1967), pp. 233-40 and 241-52. Robert Lowell has a vivid account of mutual friends in "Visiting the Tates," *Sewanee Review,* LXVII (Autumn, 1959), 557-59.

12. Eleanor Ross Taylor's verse has appeared in *Poetry* and other magazines. Randall Jarrell wrote the introduction to her one volume of poems, *Wilderness of Ladies* (New York, 1960). Mrs. Taylor is the sister of the novelists Fred E. Ross, author of *Jackson Mahaffey* (Boston, 1951), and James Ross, author of *They Don't Dance Much* (Boston, 1940).

13. "The Furnishings of a House," *Kenyon Review,* I (Summer, 1939), 308.

14. Father James Harold Flye, the friend and correspondent of James Agee, married the Taylors in the chapel of the school Agee made famous, St. Andrew's, between Monteagle and Sewanee, Tennessee.

15. The stories in the individual volumes, with their places of original publication, are listed in the Bibliography.

16. Jenice Jordan, "He 'Writes for Fun,' But His Stories Sell," *Columbus Dispatch,* December 6, 1959, book section.

Chapter Two

1. *A Long Fourth and Other Stories* (New York, 1948). All stories cited in this chapter are from this volume.

2. Kenneth Clay Cathey, in "Peter Taylor: An Evaluation," *Western Review,* XVIII (Autumn, 1953), 12-13, complains: "Unfortunately, the reader is not sure as to the specific nature of this inquiry, although we can speculate that it concerns her revaluation of the loyalties by which she has lived and which gave her existence meaning." He chides Taylor for a deliberate and unnecessary ambiguity that he thinks results from a coyness in withholding interpretation.

3. Oswald Spengler, *The Decline of the West,* trans. Charles Francis Atkinson (New York, 1961), II, 327-28.
4. *Ibid.,* 328-29.
5. *Ibid.,* 165.

Chapter Three

1. Katherine Anne Porter, Introduction to Eudora Welty's *A Curtain of Green* (New York, 1941), p. xviii.
2. *A Woman of Means* (New York, 1950). In this chapter, all page numbers in parentheses refer to this novel.
3. "Casa Anna," *Harper's Bazaar* (November, 1948), pp. 137 and 212-24; "Dudley for the Dartmouth Cup," *New Yorker,* XXV (May 28, 1949), 24-28.
4. Powers, p. 262.
5. Cathey, pp. 16-17.
6. Martin Joos, *The Five Clocks* (Bloomington, 1962).
7. Malcolm Cowley, Introduction to *Great Tales of the Deep South* (New York, 1955), pp. vii-ix.
8. See Thomas Wilcox, "A Novelist of Means," *Sewanee Review,* LIX (Winter, 1951), 151-54, for an excellent study of the meaning and the techniques in *A Woman of Means.*

Chapter Four

1. *The Widows of Thornton* (New York, 1954). All stories cited in this chapter are from this volume.
2. Peter Taylor, quoted on dust jacket of *The Widows of Thornton.*
3. Eudora Welty, "Place in Fiction," *Three Papers on Fiction* (Northampton, Mass., 1962), pp. 6 and 5.

Chapter Five

1. Cathey, pp. 14-18.
2. Dust jacket of *A Long Fourth.*
3. "The Death of a Kinsman: A Play," *Sewanee Review,* LVIII (Winter, 1949), 86-119.
4. Cathey, p. 15.
5. Morgan Blum, "Peter Taylor: Self-Limitation in Fiction," *Sewanee Review,* LXX (Autumn, 1962), 559-62.
6. Brainard Cheney, "Peter Taylor's Plays," *Sewanee Review,* LXX (Autumn, 1962), 580-82.
7. *Tennessee Day in St. Louis: A Comedy* (New York, 1957).
8. Compare the parents in "The Scoutmaster" in *A Long Fourth,* who play cards at the peak of a family crisis.

9. "A Stand in the Mountains," *Kenyon Review*, XXX ([March] 1968), 169-264.

Chapter Six

1. Though Taylor does briefly discuss his ideas on writing in a recent essay, "That Cloistered Jazz," *Michigan Quarterly Review*, V (Fall, 1966), 237-45, few details are given. "1939" and the other stories cited in this chapter are in *Happy Families Are All Alike* (New York, 1959).
2. Blum, 567-68.
3. *Ibid.*
4. Cathey, p. 10.
5. Blum, p. 562.
6. "Notes on Writing," *New Directions, 1940* (Norfolk, Connecticut, 1940), p. 203, quoted in George Hendrick, *Katherine Anne Porter* (New York, 1965), p. 15.
7. Jordan, *loc. cit.*
8. The "battle" imagery in this story is discussed by Sister Cor Mariae Schuler, "The House of Peter Taylor: Fiction and Structure" (Ph.D. dissertation, University of Notre Dame, 1964), p. 244.
9. Jordan, *loc. cit.* The city of Chatham is also the setting for "Promise of Rain." In the original magazine publication of all three Chatham stories, the city was called Mero. Chatham was the name given in the magazine publication of "A Friend and Protector" (then titled "Who Was Jesse's Friend and Protector?") to the small country town later called Braxton.
10. The Bronzino painting depicts a languorous Venus being fondled by a winged youth, while a child tossing roses and an old man with his arm outstretched protectively look on. For a reproduction, see Everard M. Upjohn and others, *History of World Art* (New York, 1949), Plate 246.
11. "Venus, Cupid, Folly and Time" was the first prize story in *Prize Stories 1959: The O. Henry Awards*, ed. Paul Engle (New York, 1959) and has been reprinted in *First Prize Stories, 1919-1963, from the O. Henry Memorial Awards*, ed. Harry Hansen (New York, 1963). It was also selected for *The Best American Short Stories*, 1959, ed. Martha Foley and David Burnett (Boston, 1959).
12. Two potentially grotesque characters in "The Other Times," the toothless three-hundred-pound tavern owner and her deaf-mute husband, become credible characters in Taylor's understated treatment of them.

Chapter Seven

1. *Miss Leonora When Last Seen and Fifteen Other Stories* (New York, 1963). All page numbers in parentheses in this chapter are references to this volume.
2. *The Collected Stories of Peter Taylor* (New York, 1969).
3. *Sewanee Review,* LXX (Autumn, 1962), 528-602.
4. See Walter Sullivan, "The Continuing Renascence: Southern Fiction in the Fifties," in *South: Modern Southern Literature in Its Cultural Setting,* ed. Louis D. Rubin, Jr., and Robert D. Jacobs (Garden City, 1961), pp. 376-91; John M. Bradbury, *Renaissance in the South: A Critical History of the Literature, 1920-1960* (Chapel Hill, 1963), p. 120; Chester E. Eisinger, *Fiction of the Forties* (Chicago, 1963), pp. 193-98; Richard K. Meeker, "The Youngest Generation of Southern Fiction Writers," in *Southern Writers: Appraisals in Our Time,* ed. R. C. Simonini, Jr. (Charlottesville, 1964), pp. 162-91; William Peden, *The American Short Story* (Boston, 1964), pp. 61-68.
5. In Eudora Welty's first short story collection, *A Curtain of Green* (1941), for instance, there were seventeen stories in a wide variety of styles; in her second volume, *A Wide Net* (1943), she limited herself to nine stories, all in much the same style.
6. Flannery O'Connor, "The Role of the Catholic Novelist," *Greyfriar: Siena Studies in Literature,* VII (1964), 7-8.
7. Blum, p. 559.
8. "A Walled Garden" (originally "Like the Sad Heart of Ruth") is the only story Taylor has passed over and then later collected.
9. Warren, p. vii.
10. "The Party," *River,* I (March, 1937), 4-8.
11. "The Lady is Civilized," *River,* I (April, 1937), 50-54.
12. "The School Girl," *American Prefaces,* VII (Spring, 1942), 272-76.
13. "Attendant Evils," *Vanderbilt Miscellany, 1919-1944,* ed. Richard Croom Beatty (Nashville, 1944), pp. 144-50.
14. "Uncles," *New Yorker,* XXV (December 17, 1949), 24-28.
15. "Nerves," *New Yorker,* XXXVII (September 16, 1961), 38-41.
16. Farrar, Straus and Giroux is the new publisher.
17. "The Elect," *McCall's,* XCV (April, 1968), 106-7, 168-69, 172.
18. "There" was included in both *Prize Stories 1965: The O. Henry Awards* (Garden City, 1965) and *The Best American Short Stories of 1965* (Boston, 1965).
19. "The Throughway," *Sewanee Review,* LXXII (Autumn, 1964), 559-78.
20. "The End of Play," *Virginia Quarterly Review,* XLI (Spring, 1965), 248-65.
21. "A Cheerful Disposition," *Sewanee Review,* LXXV (Spring, 1967), 243-65.

Chapter Eight

1. Louis D. Rubin, Jr., *The Faraway Country: Writers of the Modern South* (Seattle, 1963), pp. 236-37.
2. Louise Y. Gossett, *Violence in Recent Southern Fiction* (Durham, 1965), p. ix.
3. Tennessee Williams, Introduction to Carson McCullers' *Reflections in a Golden Eye* (New York, 1950), pp. xi-xv.
4. Peden, pp. 61-68.
5. Welty, "Place in Fiction," p. 7.
6. Warren, p. viii; Andrew Lytle, "The Displaced Family," *Sewanee Review*, LXVI (Winter, 1958), 115-20; Ashley Brown, "The Early Fiction of Peter Taylor," *Sewanee Review*, LXX (Autumn, 1962), 588-602.
7. Peden, p. 1.
8. As early as 1954, Taylor was reported working on a novel entitled "A Rope From Hell to Hang Her With," a love story set in Memphis during the Depression. This work. still in progress, is now planned as a trilogy. *A Stand in the Mountains* is the first of the series of plays Taylor is working on.
9. Henry James, "Anthony Trollope," in *The Future of the Novel*, ed. Leon Edel (New York, 1956), pp. 259-60.
10. Sullivan, p. 390.
11. Warren, p. ix.
12. James, p. 240.
13. Peden, p. 68.

Selected Bibliography

PRIMARY SOURCES

1. *Fiction and Drama* (works collected in each volume are listed in chronological order of publication; a number in parentheses at the conclusion of an entry indicates number of appearances of that work in anthologies):

A Long Fourth and Other Stories. Introduction by Robert Penn Warren. New York: Harcourt, Brace and Company, 1948.

"A Spinster's Tale," *Southern Review*, VI (Autumn, 1940), 270-92. (2)

"Sky Line," *Southern Review*, VI (Winter, 1941), 489-507. (1)

"The Fancy Woman," *Southern Review*, VII (Summer, 1941), 65-92. (5)

"Rain in the Heart," *Sewanee Review*, LIII (Winter, 1945), 23-43. (1)

"The Scoutmaster," originally "The Scout Master," *Partisan Review*, XII (Summer, 1945), 368-92. (1)

"A Long Fourth," *Sewanee Review*, LIV (Summer, 1946), 396-438. (1)

"Allegiance," *Kenyon Review*, IX (Spring, 1947), 188-200.

A Woman of Means. Illustrated by Margaret Bloy Graham. New York: Harcourt, Brace and Company, 1950. Sections of this novel published separately as short stories are: "Casa Anna," *Harper's Bazaar* (November, 1948), pp. 137, 212-24; "Dudley for the Dartmouth Cup," *New Yorker*, XXV (May 28, 1949), 24-28.

The Widows of Thornton. New York: Harcourt, Brace and Company, 1954.

"Cookie," originally "Middle Age," *New Yorker*, XXIV (November 6, 1948), 29-32.

"The Death of a Kinsman: A Play," *Sewanee Review*, LVII (Winter, 1949), 86-119.

"Porte-Cochere," *New Yorker*, XXV (July 16, 1949), 21-24. (3)

"A Wife of Nashville," *New Yorker*, XXV (December 3, 1949), 42-61. (4)

"Their Losses," *New Yorker*, XXVI (March 11, 1950), 24-30. (1)

"What You Hear From 'Em?" *New Yorker*, XXVI (February 10, 1951), 31-38. (4)

"Two Ladies in Retirement," *New Yorker*, XXVII (March 31, 1951), 26-46.

"Bad Dreams," *New Yorker*, XXVII (May 19, 1951), 32-42.

"The Dark Walk," *Harper's Bazaar*, March 1954, pp. 120-214.

Tennessee Day in St. Louis: A Comedy. New York: Random House, 1957. Act I originally published as "Tennessee Day in St. Louis," *Kenyon Review,* XVIII (Winter, 1956), 92-119.

Happy Families Are All Alike: A Collection of Stories. New York: McDowell, Obolensky, 1959.

"A Walled Garden," originally "Like the Sad Heart of Ruth," *New Republic,* CV (December 8, 1941), 783-84.

"1939," originally "A Sentimental Journey," *New Yorker,* XXXI (March 12, 1955), 33-57.

"The Other Times," *New Yorker,* XXXIII (February 23, 1957), 36-66.

"Promise of Rain," originally "The Unforgivable," *New Yorker,* XXXIII (January 25, 1958), 32-51.

"Venus, Cupid, Folly and Time," *Kenyon Review,* XX (Spring, 1958), 169-202. (5)

"Je Suis Perdu," originally "A Pair of Bright Blue Eyes," *New Yorker,* XXXIV (June 7, 1958), 33-38.

"The Little Cousins," originally "Cousins, Family Love, Family Life, All That," *New Yorker,* XXXV (April 25, 1959), 38-44.

"A Friend and Protector," originally "Who Was Jesse's Friend and Protector?" *Kenyon Review,* XXI (Summer, 1959), 395-418. (1)

"Heads of Houses," *New Yorker,* XXXV (September 12, 1959), 52-87. (1)

"Guests," *New Yorker,* XXXV (October 3, 1959), 48-89.

Miss Leonora When Last Seen and Fifteen Other Stories. New York: Ivan Obolensky, Inc., 1963. In addition to six new stories, this collection includes the following works from his earlier out-of-print volumes: "A Spinster's Tale," "Allegiance," "Sky Line," "The Fancy Woman," from *A Long Fourth*; "A Wife of Nashville," "Bad Dreams," "Cookie," "The Death of a Kinsman," "Their Losses," "What You Hear From 'Em?" from *The Widows of Thornton.*

"Miss Leonora When Last Seen," *New Yorker,* XXXVI (November 19, 1960), 52-90. (1)

"Reservations: A Love Story," *New Yorker,* XXXVII (February 25, 1961), 37-72.

"An Overwhelming Question," *Encounter,* XVIII (March, 1962), 7-15.

"At the Drugstore," *Sewanee Review,* LXX (Autumn, 1962), 528-58. (1)

"A Strange Story," originally "Demons," *New Yorker,* XXXIX (August 24, 1963), 30-63.

"Two Pilgrims," *New Yorker,* XXXIX (September 7, 1963), 36-42. (1)

The Collected Stories of Peter Taylor. New York: Farrar, Straus and Giroux, 1969. In addition to five new stories, this collection includes the following works from his earlier out-of-print volumes: "A Spinster's Tale," "The Fancy Woman," from *A Long Fourth*; "Their Losses," "What You Hear From 'Em?", "A Wife of Nashville," "Cookie," from *The Widows of Thornton*; "The Other Times," "Venus, Cupid, Folly and Time," "1939," "Guests," "Heads of Houses," "*Je Suis Perdu*," from *Happy Families;* "Reservations," "At the Drugstroe," "Two Pilgrims," "Miss Leonora When Last Seen," from *Miss Leonora.*

"There," *Kenyon Review*, XXVI (Winter, 1964), 144-70. (2)

"Mrs. Billingsby's Wine," *New Yorker*, XLIII (October 14, 1967), 56-60.

"The Elect," *McCall's*, XCV (April, 1968), 106-7, 168-69, 172.

"First Heat," *Shenandoah*, XIX (Winter, 1968), 28-36.

"Dean of Men," *Virginia Quarterly Review, XLV* (Spring, 1969), 258-93.

2. *Uncollected Fiction:*

"The Party," *River*, I (March, 1937), 4-8.

"The Lady is Civilized," *River*, I (April, 1937), 50-54.

"The School Girl," *American Prefaces*, VII (Spring, 1942), 272-76.

"Attendant Evils," in *Vanderbilt Miscellany, 1919-1944*, ed. Richard Croom Beatty. Nashville: Vanderbilt University Press, 1944.

"Uncles," *New Yorker*, XXV (December 17, 1949), 24-28.

"Nerves," *New Yorker*, XXXVII (September 16, 1961), 38-41.

"The Throughway," *Sewanee Review*, LXXII (Autumn, 1964), 559-78.

"The End of Play," *Virginia Quarterly Review*, XLI (Spring, 1965), 248-65.

"A Cheerful Disposition," *Sewanee Review*, LXXV (Spring, 1967), 243-65.

"Tom, Tell Him," *Sewanee Review*, LXXVI (Spring, 1968), 159-86.

"Daphne's Lover," *Sewanee Review*, LXXVII (Spring, 1969), 225-50.

3. *Miscellaneous Works:*

"The Furnishings of a House," *Kenyon Review*, I (Summer, 1939), 308. [Verse.]

"Tribute at Yale," *Alumni News* [University of North Carolina at Greensboro], LIV (Spring, 1966), 2-5. [Essay.]

"That Cloistered Jazz," *Michigan Quarterly Review*, V (Fall, 1966), 237-45. Revised version reprinted as "Randall Jarrell," in *Randall Jarrell, 1914-1965*, ed. Robert Lowell, Peter Taylor, and

ROBERT PENN WARREN. New York: Farrar, Straus & Giroux, 1967. [Essay.]

"A Stand in the Mountains," *Kenyon Review,* XXX (March 1968), 169-264. [Play.]

SECONDARY SOURCES

1. *Bibliographical:*

SMITH, JAMES PENNY. "A Peter Taylor Checklist," *Critique,* IX, 3 (1967), 31-36.

2. *Biographical:*

ETHRIDGE, JAMES M. and BARBARA KOPALA (eds.). "Taylor, Peter (Hillsman) 1919- ." *Contemporary Authors.* Vol. XV-XVI. Detroit: Gale Research Company, 1966. Most up-to-date of the sketches in standard reference works.

Joint Committee of the North Carolina English Teachers Association and the North Carolina Library Association. "Taylor, Peter." *North Carolina Authors: A Selective Handbook.* Chapel Hill: University of North Carolina Library, 1952. (Extension Publication, XVIII, no. 1.) First-person capsule biography of about 175 words.

JORDAN, JENICE. "He 'Writes for Fun,' But His Stories Sell," *Columbus Dispatch,* December 6, 1959, book section. Short profile of Taylor as Ohio State University professor, as writer, and as frustrated artist and handy-man; describes his schedule and his habits in writing.

KUNITZ, STANLEY J. and HOWARD HAYCRAFT. "Taylor, Peter Hillsman." *Twentieth Century Authors: First Supplement.* New York: H. W. Wilson, 1955. Brief and vague in details.

3. *General Criticism:*

BLUM, MORGAN. "Peter Taylor: Self-Limitation in Fiction," *Sewanee Review,* LXX (Autumn, 1962), 559-78. Best general essay on Taylor; excellent delineation of self-imposed boundaries within which Taylor writes and of artistic accomplishment made within these boundaries.

BRADBURY, JOHN M. *Renaissance in the South: A Critical History of the Literature, 1920-1960.* Chapel Hill: University of North Carolina Press, 1963. Finds Taylor "basically in sympathy with the agrarian tradition."

BROWN, ASHLEY. "The Early Fiction of Peter Taylor," *Sewanee Review,* LXX (Autumn, 1962), 588-602. Appreciation of *A Woman of Means* and several stories in *A Long Fourth*; sees Taylor as "essentially ironic about history" and not dependent on Faulknerian myth of the South.

CATHEY, KENNETH CLAY. "Peter Taylor: An Evaluation," *Western Review,* XVIII (Autumn, 1953), 9-19. First major essay on Taylor; stresses his obvious promise, his narrow range, and his steady improvement.

CHENEY, BRAINARD. "Peter Taylor's Plays," *Sewanee Review,* LXX (Autumn, 1962), 579-87. Only full discussion of Taylor's two published plays; finds his playwriting a "paradox" because it attempts to realize the objectives of fiction on the stage. Should be compared to Andrew Lytle's essay listed below under reviews of *Tennessee Day*.

EISINGER, CHESTER E. "Andrew Lytle and Peter Taylor: Conservative Fiction in Tennessee." *Fiction of the Forties*. Chicago: University of Chicago Press, 1963. Notes Taylor's relationship to Henry James in method and to Lytle and Carolyn Gordon in theme.

MEEKER, RICHARD K. "The Youngest Generation of Southern Fiction Writers." *Southern Writers: Appraisals in Our Time,* ed. R. C. SIMONINI, JR. Charlottesville: University Press of Virginia, 1965. Calls Taylor "the most distinguished product" of the second-generation Vanderbilt school.

NYREN, DOROTHY (ed.). "Taylor, Peter (1917-)." *A Library of Literary Criticism: Modern American Literature*. New York: Frederick Unger, 1960. Collection of brief extracts from reviews.

PEDEN, WILLIAM. *The American Short Story*. Boston: Houghton, Mifflin, 1964. Excellent assessment of Taylor's chief merits.

SCHULER, SISTER COR MARIAE [BARBARA]. "The House of Peter Taylor: Vision and Structure." Unpublished Ph.D. dissertation, University of Notre Dame, 1964. Available on University Microfilm 64-10, 499. Good overall study, analyzing separately Taylor's use of setting, characterization, theme, and technique; relates all Taylor's work to central image of the "house." For brief presentation of some of the same ideas, see Barbara Schuler, "The House of Peter Taylor," *Critique,* IX, 3 (1967), 6-18.

SMITH, JAMES Penny. "Narration and Theme in Taylor's *A Woman of Means,*" *Critique,* IX, 3 (1967), 19-30. Analysis of identity theme.

SULLIVAN, WALTER, "The Continuing Renascence: Southern Fiction in the Fifties." *South: Modern Southern Literature in Its Cultural Setting,* ed. LOUIS D. RUBIN, JR. and ROBERT D. JACOBS. Garden

City: Doubleday (Dolphin Books), 1961. Bibliography by JAMES B. MERIWETHER. Shows how Taylor and other recent Southern writers represent a change in the Southern temper.

WARREN, ROBERT PENN. Introduction to *A Long Fourth and Other Stories*. New York: Harcourt, Brace and Company, 1948. Laudatory essay which launched Taylor's career and determined the issues and the tone for most later criticism.

WEST, RAY B., JR. *The Short Story in America.* New York: Gateway Editions, 1952. Discussion of short story writers of the 1940's, with scattered references to Taylor.

4. *Selected Reviews*:

A. *A Long Fourth and Other Stories.*

Commonweal, XLVIII (June 25, 1948), 262-63. (J. F. Powers)
Hudson Review, I (Summer, 1948), 276-88. (Joseph Frank)
Kenyon Review, XI (Winter, 1949), 162-64. (Isa Kapp)
Nashville Banner, April 26, 1948, p. 26. (Frances Cheney)
New Republic, CXVIII (March 8, 1948), 25-26. (John Farrelly)
New York Herald Tribune Weekly Book Review, March 14, 1948, p. 5. (Coleman Rosenberger)
New York Times, March 4, 1948, p. 23.
New York Times Book Review, March 21, 1948, p. 6. (Hubert Creekmore)
New Yorker, XXIV (March 13, 1948), 110.
Saturday Review of Literature, XXI (March 27, 1948), 17-18. (Marjorie Brace)

B. *A Woman of Means.*

Chicago Sunday Tribune, May 14, 1950, p. 7. (Paul Engle)
Commonweal, LII (June 23, 1950), 275. (George Miles)
Kenyon Review, XII (Autumn, 1950), 730-34. (Denham Sutcliffe)
Manchester Guardian, November 24, 1950, p. 4. (Elizabeth Jenkins)
New Republic, CXXII (June 26, 1950), 20. (James Stern)
New Statesman & Nation, XL (December 2, 1950), 566. (Robert Kee)
New York Herald Tribune Book Review, May 21, 1950, p. 10. (Coleman Rosenberger)
New York Times, May 19, 1950, p. 25.
New York Times Book Review, June 11, 1950, p. 8. (Robert Penn Warren)
New Yorker, XXVI (May 20, 1950), 106.
Saturday Review of Literature, XXXIII (June 3, 1950), 13. (Evelyn Eaton)
Sewanee Review, LIX (Winter, 1951), 151-54. (Thomas Wilcox)
Time, LV (May 15, 1950), 110.

Western Review, XVI (Autumn, 1951), 87-88. (Roger Shattuck)
Yale Review, XXXIX (Summer, 1950), 765-68. (Paul Pickrel)

C. *The Widows of Thornton.*

Arizona Quarterly, X (Autumn, 1954), 282. (Mary E. Lauver)
Chicago Sunday Tribune, May 31, 1954, p. 4. (Paul Engle)
Commonweal, LXI (December 17, 1954), 317. (Richard Hayes)
New York Herald Tribune Book Review, May 2, 1954, p. 4. (Dan Wickenden)
New York Times, June 29, 1954, p. 25.
New York Times Book Review, May 2, 1954, p. 5. (Frank H. Lyell)
San Francisco Chronicle, May 13, 1954, p. 19. (D. R. McDaniels)
Saturday Review, XXXVII (May 8, 1954), 14. (Mack Morriss)
Sewanee Review, LXIII (Winter, 1955), 137-44. (Thomas Mabry)
Shenandoah, VI (Winter, 1954), 73-78. (Marvin Mudrick)

D. *Tennessee Day in St. Louis.*

Sewanee Review, LXVI (Winter, 1958), 115-31. (Andrew Lytle)

E. *Happy Families Are All Alike.*

Chicago Sunday Tribune, December 6, 1959, p. 12. (Richard Sullivan)
Christian Science Monitor, December 24, 1959, p. 7. (Ruth Blackman)
Commonweal, LXXI (January 1, 1960), 401. (Max Cosman)
Esquire, March, 1960, p. 60. (Dorothy Parker)
Kenyon Review, XXII (Winter, 1960), 167. ([Irving Kreutz])
Manchester Guardian and Evening News, August 19, 1960, p. 5. (Norman Schrapnel)
Minnesota Review, I (Fall, 1960), 115-21. (W. Stuckey)
New Statesman, LX (August 6, 1960), 192. (Jeremy Brooks)
New York Herald Tribune Book Review, December 6, 1959, p. 9. (Gene Baro)
New York Times, January 12, 1960, p. 45. (William DuBois)
New York Times Book Review, November 22, 1959, p. 4. (Frank H. Lyell)
San Francisco Chronicle, December 6, 1959, p. 39. (Charles Morgan)
Saturday Review, November 28, 1959, p. 33. (William Peden)
Times Literary Supplement (London), August 19, 1960, p. 525.
Virginia Quarterly Review, XXXVI (Spring, 1960), xl.

F. *Miss Leonora When Last Seen.*

Book Week, March 8, 1964, p. 11. (Glendy Culligan)
Chicago Sunday Tribune, April 5, 1964, p. 4. (Richard Sullivan)
New York Review of Books, II (June 11, 1964), 11. (John Thompson)
New York Times Book Review, March 29, 1964, p. 4. (Gene Baro)
Saturday Review, May 16, 1964, p. 45. (Lewis Leary)

Sewanee Review, LXXIII (Winter, 1965), 106-19. (T. A. Hanzo)
Time, LXXXIII (March 13, 1964), 107.
Virginia Quarterly Review, XL (Summer, 1964), civ.

G. *The Collected Stories of Peter Taylor.*

Christian Science Monitor, January 22, 1970, p. 7. (Keith M. Opdahl)
Commonweal, XCI (February 6, 1970), 516-18. (Albert J. Griffith)
Harper's, CCXXXIX (November, 1969), 130, 134. (John Thompson)
Nation, CCIX (October 20, 1969), 418-19. (Robert K. Morris)
New Republic, CLXI (October 18, 1969), 29. (Barbara Raskin)
New York Times Book Review, October 19, 1969, pp. 4, 26. (Richard Howard)
Newsweek, LXXIV (October 20, 1969), 121-22. (Geoffrey Wolff)
Saturday Review, LII (October 18, 1969), 40. (William C. Hamlin)

Index